John

Dwelling in God's Word

John

The Light Revealed, the Darkness Resisted:
A Fifty-Day Devotional

GRAHAM JOSEPH HILL

Eagna Publishing • Sydney, Australia

JOHN
The Light Revealed, the Darkness Resisted: A Fifty-Day Devotional

Published by: Eagna Publishing (Sydney, Australia)
eagnapublishing@icloud.com
Cover and interior design: Graham Joseph Hill
www.grahamjosephhill.com

paperback isbn: 978-1-7641791-2-6
ebook isbn: 978-1-7641791-3-3
version number 2025-11-04

NATIONAL LIBRARY OF AUSTRALIA

A catalogue record for this book is available from the National Library of Australia

Contents

Introduction 1

Day 1: The Word Made Flesh 4

Day 2: The Voice in the Wilderness 6

Day 3: Come and See 8

Day 4: Abundance Hidden in Obedience 10

Day 5: The Disrupting Christ 12

Day 6: Born Again into Light 15

Day 7: He Must Increase 18

Day 8: The Thirst Beneath All Thirsts 21

Day 9: Harvest in Unexpected Fields 24

Day 10: Faith That Goes Beyond Signs 26

Day 11: Do You Want to Be Made Well? 28

Day 12: The Works of the Father 31

Day 13: The Bread That Breaks Open Trust 33

Day 14: Fear and the Voice Over the Waves 35

Day 15: The Bread That Offends and Satisfies 38

Day 16: The Offense and the Clinging 40

Day 17: Hiddenness and Holy Boldness 42

Day 18: Thirst and Division 45

Day 19: Stones Dropped, Mercy Written 47

Day 20: Light for Those Who Will Follow 49

Day 21: Before Abraham Was, I AM 51

Day 22: Mud, Spit, and Sight 54

Day 23: Eyes Opened, Hearts Exposed 56

Day 24: The Voice of the Shepherd 58

Day 25: Held in the Hand of God 60

Day 26: The Weeping God and the Grave Unsealed 62

Day 27: Plotting Death Against Life 64

Day 28: Fragrance That Fills the House 66

Day 29: The Glory of a Dying Seed 69

Day 30: Light That Won't Be Silenced 71

Day 31: The Towel, the Basin, and the Betrayer 73

Day 32: The Betrayal Foretold, the Denial Exposed 75

Day 33: The Way, the Truth, and the Homecoming 77

Day 34: The Spirit Who Comes to Stay 79

Day 35: Abide and Bear Fruit 81

Day 36: Hated but Held 83

Day 37: Sorrow, Spirit, and the Truth That Sets Free 85

Day 38: Sorrow That Turns to Joy 87

Day 39: Glory in the Hour of the Cross 89

Day 40: Kept in the Name 92

Day 41: The Glory That Makes Us One 94

Day 42: The Garden, the Trial, and the Rooster's Cry 96

Day 43: A Kingdom Not of This World 98

Day 44: The Crown, the Cross, and the Final Gift 100

Day 45: It Is Finished 102

Day 46: The First Word of Resurrection 104

Day 47: Peace in the Locked Room 107

Day 48: The Touch of Faith 110

Day 49: Breakfast at the Shore 113

Day 50: Restored by Love 116

Appendix 1: Would You Help? 119

Appendix 2: About Me 120

Appendix 3: Connect With Me 121

Introduction

This devotional is part of a larger pilgrimage through Scripture, shepherded by Rev. Dr. Graham Joseph Hill, as he walks with readers from Genesis to Revelation. The Dwelling in God's Word series (both podcast and written reflections) invites you to discover how each book of the Bible speaks to the deep longings of the soul and the demands of our shared life in the world. It's not merely a reading plan; it's a sacred journey of formation and transformation. Here, the biblical narrative meets everyday discipleship in prayerful and practical ways.

The Gospel of John shimmers with mystery, intimacy, and divine revelation. It's a Gospel for seekers and skeptics, for lovers of beauty and wrestlers with doubt, and for those aching to encounter not just teachings about God but the very heartbeat of God. John offers no birth narrative, no parables in the traditional sense. Instead, it opens with poetry and light, sweeping us into a cosmic story that pierces the ordinary with glory. Here, the eternal Word becomes flesh, and heaven stoops low enough to touch.

John's Jesus doesn't merely perform signs; he reveals signs of the Father's love. He speaks in layered metaphors, inviting the thirsty, the blind, the shamed, and the curious to abide, believe, and be born anew. This Gospel pulses with divine intimacy: meals shared, feet washed, tears shed, prayers whispered. It's less a chronology than a deep dive into the mystery of divine love unveiled in Christ.

From Cana to Calvary, from whispered midnight conversations to public confrontations, John invites us to see and be seen, to gaze upon the crucified and risen One and find life in his name. This is the Gospel of belovedness, of abiding presence, of light that no darkness can overcome. And at the center of it all is Jesus, the Lamb of God, the Bread of Life, the True Vine: the One who calls each of us by name into eternal, abundant, radiant life.

This devotional is rooted in the richness of the biblical text and nourished by careful theological reflection. It invites you to sit with Scripture: slowly, reverently, attentively. Each entry draws you deeper into John's Gospel, exposing overlooked treasures and summoning fresh faith. But this isn't just about knowing more. It's about living differently. As you journey through these pages, you'll be challenged to embrace justice, embody mercy, cultivate humility, and become a participant in the reconciling mission of God.

These reflections don't avoid hard questions or flatten the text into sentiment. They dare to wrestle. To pray. To imagine. And they call you to more than contemplation. They invite you to action: to live the Gospel in your neighborhood, your body, your workplace, your church.

As you immerse yourself in this devotional, may your theology deepen, your heart soften, and your hands be ready to serve. May these fifty days in John stir something courageous in you: a longing to see and be seen by the living Christ.

How to Use This Devotional:

1. This book leads you through the Gospel of John in fifty short devotions.

2. You're encouraged to pair this with the companion podcast: https://grahamjosephhill.com/devotions.

3. Each day, you are invited to:

a. Read the passage slowly, letting it read you.

b. Sit with the day's devotion and let its truths sink deep.

c. Pray, honestly and vulnerably, into the text.

d. Discern one concrete action in response.

Whether you read alone, with family, or within a community, this journey through John will shape your heart and stretch your faith. Come ready to be changed.

Day 1: The Word Made Flesh

Reading: John 1:1–18

In the beginning (before time, before breath, before history), there was the Word. Not an idea, not a distant decree, but a living, divine Being. The Word was with God. The Word was God. The Gospel of John begins not with genealogy or angels but with mystery: eternity speaking itself into creation.

Through this Word, everything came into being. Light pierced the void. Order was born from chaos. Every leaf, every heartbeat, every breath carries the echo of this Word's creative power. And yet, the world didn't recognize its source. The light shines, but darkness still clings.

Then comes the scandal: "The Word became flesh." Not simply visiting. Not hovering above, but entering skin, bone, blood, vulnerability. The infinite wrapped in fragility. Glory hidden inside poverty. The Creator is breathing dust. This isn't how empires expect gods to act. This isn't how power usually operates. But this is the way of God.

John declares that this Word came full of grace and truth. Not balancing the two but pouring out both in full measure. Grace that bends low. Truth that stands firm. Together, they form the strange, beautiful tension that defines the life of Christ and the life of his followers.

The world didn't recognize him. His people rejected him. But to those who did receive him, he gave the right to become children of God: born not of bloodline, not of status, not of human effort, but of divine gift. Adoption into the very life of God.

4

This is the core of discipleship: not self-made identity but received belonging. In a culture addicted to achievement, performance, and curated identity, the Gospel of John dares to proclaim that true life is a gift. We don't climb into grace. We are welcomed into it.

And so, we, too, are called into this strange way of incarnation. To live as those who carry the light into the dark places. To embody grace and truth in a world allergic to both. To resist the temptation to wield power as the world does and instead stoop low in love.

The Word made flesh doesn't invite us into escapism. It calls us into embodied faith: into neighborhoods, injustices, friendships, failures, and fragile beauty. Christ moves into the neighborhood, so must we.

Here, at the beginning of John's Gospel, we aren't given simple answers. We are given presence. Light shining. Flesh dwelling. Glory veiled and unveiled.

And still, the Word speaks.

Guiding Truth: The Word became flesh so that we might carry the light of grace and truth into the world's darkest places.

Reflection: Where am I tempted to seek a disembodied, distant spirituality instead of an incarnate, embodied faith? How might Jesus be calling me to live His grace and truth in places of tension and vulnerability?

Prayer: Living Word, take on flesh in me. Help me carry your light into the ordinary and the broken. Teach me to embody grace without compromise and truth without cruelty. Dwell within me as you dwelt among us. Amen.

Day 2: The Voice in the Wilderness

Reading: John 1:19–34

The religious leaders come with questions. They don't come seeking transformation; they come seeking clarification, categories, and control. "Who are you?" they demand of John. Are you the Messiah? Elijah? The Prophet? They want a label to manage, a name to regulate, a figure they can fit into their religious scaffolding.

John refuses every title. He won't become what they want. "I'm not the Messiah." "I'm not Elijah." "I'm not the Prophet." His identity isn't found in titles but in his task. "I'm the voice of one crying out in the wilderness: make straight the way of the Lord." He isn't the light. He's the echo pointing to it.

This is the scandal of John's ministry: he refuses to make himself central. In a world obsessed with self-promotion, platform-building, and personal brands, John points away from himself. "He must increase; I must decrease." His greatness lies in his self-emptying.

When Jesus appears, John's words ring with awe: "Behold, the Lamb of God, who takes away the sin of the world." Not just a personal savior but the sacrificial Lamb for the whole world's ache, injustice, and rebellion. This is the language of Passover, of deliverance, of blood smeared on doorposts so death might pass over. But now, the Lamb walks willingly toward the cross.

John testifies that the Spirit descends and remains on Jesus. The Spirit doesn't merely visit, as with prophets of old. It stays. This is the anointed One: The Messiah who doesn't rise on armies or crowns but enters through waters of repentance, clothed in humility.

For us, this passage is a confrontation with ego and vocation. We are constantly tempted to become messiahs of our own making: to save ourselves, to rescue others on our terms, to build significance through attention. But John calls us to a different path: to be voices, not messiahs. To bear witness, not to dominate. To prepare the way, not to become the way.

This kind of life requires deep humility. It demands that we relinquish our hunger for recognition and allow Christ to take center stage. It also confronts our assumptions about power. The Lamb of God subverts every notion of strength that dominates our culture. Strength comes not through violence but through sacrificial love. Victory comes not through domination but through surrender.

John's witness invites us to locate our identity in relation to Jesus, not ourselves. To be voices that clear the way. To see the Lamb and name him, even when the world refuses to recognize his beauty.

And like John, we too are called to say: "I have seen, and I testify."

Guiding Truth: The disciple's vocation isn't self-promotion but witness: to decrease so that Christ may increase.

Reflection: Where am I tempted to build my name instead of pointing to Christ? How might my life more clearly reflect the Lamb who takes away the world's sin?

Prayer: Lamb of God, take away my pride. Please make me a voice that points beyond myself. Let my witness be clear, humble, and bold. May I lose myself in your beauty and find my life in your mercy. Amen.

Day 3: Come and See

Reading: John 1:35–51

The story unfolds like a quiet revolution. John stands with two of his disciples. Jesus passes by. John doesn't shout. He says: "Behold, the Lamb of God." The simplicity is striking. No spectacle. No strategy. Just a finger pointing away from self toward Christ. And immediately, two men follow.

Jesus turns to them with a question that echoes across centuries: "What are you seeking?" He doesn't begin with demands or explanations. He invites desire. Not what do you believe? But what do you long for? Discipleship starts not in the intellect but in the ache of the heart.

Their answer seems almost evasive: "Rabbi, where are you staying?" But perhaps it's the most honest reply. They don't want information. They want presence. They want to be near him, to dwell where he dwells.

Jesus answers with an invitation that still resounds: "Come and see." Not a lecture. Not a blueprint. An invitation into the unfolding mystery. Discipleship isn't built on answers but on nearness.

Andrew, after spending time with Jesus, immediately brings his brother Simon. And here, Jesus does something beautiful. He sees Simon not for who he has been but for who he'll become. "You shall be called Cephas." A new name, a new future. Discipleship is always about transformation.

The pattern continues. Philip is found. Nathanael is invited. When Nathanael doubts, Philip repeats the words of Jesus: "Come and see." Nathanael's skepticism dissolves in the face of the encounter. Jesus sees him under the fig tree: a poetic gesture of divine knowing. Nathanael moves from doubt to declaration: "You are the Son of God."

And Jesus promises more. "You will see greater things . . . angels ascending and descending on the Son of Man." A new Jacob's ladder. Heaven touches earth in the body of Christ.

This passage teaches us that discipleship begins not with perfect understanding but with movement. With desire. With being seen. With walking after Jesus before having all the answers. It shows us a Messiah who doesn't coerce but calls. Who sees potential where others see only the past? Who invites us to bring others, not by argument but by witness: "Come and see."

In a world obsessed with quick fixes and certainty, this passage invites us to cultivate a patient, relational, and embodied faith. A faith that walks alongside makes space for questions that trust encounters more than argument.

Discipleship isn't a program. It's following the voice that turns, looks us in the eye, and asks: What are you seeking?

Guiding Truth: Jesus doesn't demand certainty but invites desire; discipleship begins with the courage to follow and see.

Reflection: Where am I trying to replace a relationship with certainty? How might I invite others into the mystery of Christ with the simple words: Come and see?

Prayer: Jesus, Rabbi, and Lamb turn toward me again. Ask me what I seek and help me follow your voice. Teach me to invite others not with argument but with witness. Let my life say: Come and see. Amen.

Day 4: Abundance Hidden in Obedience

Reading: John 2:1–12

The wedding runs out of wine. It's a small crisis but a profoundly human one. In a culture where hospitality is honor, empty jars speak of shame, failure, and loss of face. This is where Jesus performs his first sign: not in a temple or courtroom but at a vulnerable feast.

Mary turns to her Son. She doesn't demand; she names the need: "They have no more wine." And Jesus responds with words that sound like resistance: "My hour hasn't yet come." Yet Mary persists, not by pleading but by trusting. She turns to the servants: "Do whatever he tells you." It's one of the most profound statements of discipleship in all of Scripture: simple, surrendered, daring.

Jesus tells the servants to fill the ceremonial jars with water. These aren't wine jars; they're for ritual cleansing. Vessels of religious purity are now filled to the brim with ordinary water, about to become vessels of extravagant joy. In this small act, Jesus transforms not only the moment but the very structures of religious expectation. The jars of cleansing become containers of celebration. Law gives way to grace.

And when the steward tastes the water-now-wine, he marvels. The best is saved for last. This is the kingdom breaking in: not scarcity, but abundance. Not duty, but delight. The Messiah begins his public ministry not by condemning sinners but by prolonging joy.

This passage speaks into our spiritual lives with quiet power. We often look for God in grand gestures, but the first miracle is hidden in ordinary obedience. The servants fill jars with water. They don't know the plan. They aren't promised anything. They obey without seeing. And somewhere in the filling, somewhere in the carrying, somewhere in the waiting, the water becomes wine.

The way of Jesus still works like this. Transformation rarely begins with spectacle. It starts with quiet, faithful acts: listening, praying, serving, and showing up repeatedly when no miracle seems near. We fill the jars. He turns them into abundance.

This story also confronts our cultural obsession with control and performance. The world says: manage, measure, secure the outcome. But Jesus invites us into mystery. Into trust. Into a life where obedience precedes understanding.

It matters that Jesus performs his first sign at a wedding feast. The kingdom of God isn't a joyless religion. It's a feast where shame is covered, honor is restored, and grace flows freely. The best wine is still being poured. The feast has only begun.

Guiding Truth: God's abundance often flows through hidden obedience: small acts of trust become vessels of extravagant grace.

Reflection: Where am I being called to simple obedience, even without seeing the outcome? How might Jesus be inviting me to exchange scarcity for the abundance of his grace?

Prayer: Jesus, true Bridegroom, teach me to trust you in the hidden places. Let my obedience become an empty vessel for your transforming grace. Turn my water into wine, my fear into joy, my smallness into your abundance. Amen.

Day 5: The Disrupting Christ

Reading: John 2:13–25

Jesus enters the temple, and he doesn't come gently.

The outer courts, meant for prayer and welcome, have become a marketplace. Tables groan under the weight of coins. Animals shuffle and cry. The air is thick with the transaction. The sacred has been swallowed by commerce. Profit disguises itself as piety.

But Jesus won't be silent. He weaves a whip from cords. He drives out the merchants and animals. Coins scatter. Tables crash. Voices shout. The calm veneer of religion is torn open. This isn't the domesticated Jesus of soft portraits. This is the Christ who refuses to let God's house be desecrated by greed and exploitation.

The disciples watch, stunned. Later, they'll remember the words of Scripture: "Zeal for your house will consume me." The Messiah's love burns hot. He isn't indifferent to the corruption of worship. He isn't passive before systems that oppress in the name of God.

When challenged, Jesus speaks in riddles: "Destroy this temple, and I will raise it again in three days." The leaders scoff: forty-six years of building, they say. But Jesus isn't speaking of stone and mortar. He speaks of his own body. His crucifixion and resurrection will become the new center of worship. The temple that truly houses God won't be built by human hands but by divine sacrifice.

This passage confronts us sharply. It forces us to examine the ways we've allowed faith to become transactional, worship to become performative, and ministry to become business-like. We've learned to package the sacred, monetize devotion, and turn prayer into a product. But Jesus still walks into these temples with fire in his eyes.

For our spiritual lives, this story isn't just about ancient corruption; it's about the living Christ who continues to overturn tables in our hearts. Where have we grown comfortable with compromised worship? Where have we let efficiency replace reverence? Where have we sold intimacy for success?

Jesus calls us back to a holy zeal: a passion for purity that isn't about perfectionism but about love. Love that refuses to share space with exploitation. Love that can't coexist with injustice. Love that demands the whole heart.

And yet, even here, Jesus offers himself as the new temple. He doesn't simply clear out the old; he becomes the meeting place between God and humanity. The cross becomes the new threshold: the resurrection, the new sanctuary.

As disciples, we are invited into this same fierce, humble posture. To welcome Christ's disruption in our own lives. To allow him to overturn what we've built on selfish ambition. To become people whose worship is costly, truthful, and free.

This is the way of the Cross-shaped life. A temple torn down. A temple raised.

Guiding Truth: Jesus disrupts corrupted worship to draw us back into the fierce holiness of communion with God.

Reflection: Where has my faith become transactional rather than transformational? What tables in my life is Jesus longing to overturn?

Prayer: Christ who cleanses the temple, enter my heart with holy fire. Drive out what dishonors your presence. Make my life a dwelling place of truth, humility, and reverent joy. Let my worship be pure and undivided. Amen.

Day 6: Born Again into Light

Reading: John 3:1–21

Nicodemus comes under cover of night. A respected teacher, a man of influence, trained in the law, and fluent in the rituals of faith. Yet something haunts him: this Jesus who heals on the Sabbath, who speaks with unschooled authority, whose words pierce through established certainties. Nicodemus carries questions, but fear tugs at him. So, he comes when the streets are quiet.

Jesus doesn't answer Nicodemus' questions. Instead, he disorients him with a deeper invitation: "Very truly I tell you, no one can see the kingdom of God unless they are born again." Not refinement. Not improvement. Not a polishing of religious credentials. But birth: violent, messy, entirely new.

Nicodemus stumbles. "How can this be?" he asks, caught between literalism and longing. But Jesus presses on. The Spirit moves like the wind: untamed, uncontained. The new birth isn't managed. It's received. It's surrender, not mastery.

Jesus lifts Nicodemus beyond theological debate into mystery. "Just as Moses lifted the snake in the wilderness, so the Son of Man must be lifted." Healing will come not through avoidance of pain but through facing it: looking upon the crucified Christ, lifted high, bearing the poison of sin so that all who look may live.

And then come the words that have echoed across centuries: "For God so loved the world . . . "Love isn't reserved for the clean or the deserving. Love that enters broken systems, fractured hearts, and violent histories. Love that gives. Love that bleeds.

But light brings judgment. Not because God delights in condemnation but because people love darkness. Darkness feels safe to those addicted to control, secrecy, and self-made righteousness. Light exposes. Light heals. But it also confronts.

For our spiritual lives, this passage calls us into radical vulnerability. The new birth isn't a religious badge; it's a death and a resurrection. It invites us to lay down every identity we've built for ourselves (status, knowledge, reputation) and receive an identity rooted in divine grace.

Discipleship shaped by this truth doesn't fear exposure. It welcomes the Spirit's wind, even when it disrupts. It longs for light, even when it wounds. It dares to live publicly surrendered rather than privately self-protected.

In a culture obsessed with image management, self-preservation, and curated spirituality, Jesus still invites us into something wilder: rebirth. The kingdom isn't entered through effort but through yielding. The cross stands lifted not only as a symbol of salvation but as an invitation into this cruciform life.

Nicodemus came in the night. But the light had already begun to find him.

Guiding Truth: The way into the kingdom isn't an improvement but surrender: a new birth through grace that welcomes light and releases control.

Reflection: Where am I still trying to manage my life rather than surrender to rebirth? What part of me resists the light Christ offers, fearing what may be exposed?

Prayer: Spirit who moves like wind breathes new life into me. Strip away my need for control. Help me walk into your light unafraid, trusting that what you expose, you will heal. Birth me again into your grace. Amen.

Day 7: He Must Increase

Reading: John 3:22–36

A dispute arises: a small argument between John's disciples and a fellow Jew about ceremonial washing. But beneath the surface simmers something deeper: anxiety, comparison, fear. They come to John, worried. "Rabbi, that man who was with you on the other side of the Jordan, the one you testified about: look, he is baptizing, and everyone is going to him!"

This is the ancient ache of rivalry: the fear of being eclipsed. The hunger for status is disguised as concern for loyalty. We see it in religious circles, ministries, politics, and families. The fear that someone else's rising light will dim our own.

But John's response is striking. He doesn't defend his platform. He doesn't panic. He rests. "A person can receive only what is given from heaven." His identity isn't self-constructed. It's received. His role was always preparatory: he wasn't the groom but the friend of the groom. And now that the bridegroom has come, John's joy is complete.

Then come the words that have become a banner for every disciple: "He must increase; I must decrease." Not as self-hatred but as joyful surrender. John's greatness is found in stepping aside, in becoming smaller so that Christ might be magnified.

The text shifts into a deeper reflection. "The one who comes from above is above all," Jesus speaks the words of God because the Spirit rests upon him without measure. He isn't merely another teacher in the long chain of prophets; he is the Word himself. Those who receive his testimony affirm that God is faithful.

But there's also a sobering line: "Whoever rejects the Son won't see life, for God's wrath remains on them." This isn't vindictive. It's reality. To reject the One who embodies life is to remain in death. Light has come, but some still choose darkness.

For our spiritual lives, this passage confronts the hidden places where we seek to be at the center. Where we quietly measure our worth against others. Where we turn ministry into competition or friendship into rivalry, in a culture obsessed with visibility, self-promotion, and constant comparison, John's words strike like lightning: It isn't about us. It never was.

The freedom John exhibits is radical. He is free from the addiction to applause. Free from the grasping to remain relevant. Free from the need to defend his role. His identity is rooted not in crowds but in calling. His joy is complete because Christ has come.

For us, true discipleship is the slow, painful, beautiful journey of decreasing: letting ego diminish, letting our small kingdoms dissolve so that the glory of Christ might take center stage.

John the Baptist teaches us that joy grows best in surrender. That the way up is always down. That greatness is found in losing ourselves in the radiance of the Lamb.

Guiding Truth: The path of true discipleship is joyful surrender: he must increase; we must decrease.

Reflection: Where am I still clinging to my platform rather than yielding to Christ's glory? How might my joy grow deeper as I step aside and let Christ become greater?

Prayer: Jesus, Lamb of God, teach me the freedom of surrender. Diminish my ego, quiet my striving, and center my life on you alone. May my joy be complete as you increase in me. Amen.

Day 8: The Thirst Beneath All Thirsts

Reading: John 4:1–26

Jesus sits by a well at noon. The sun scalds, the earth shimmers. His disciples have gone for food. Alone, tired, and thirsty, this is how the Son of God chooses to meet a woman whom her neighbors have rejected, and perhaps by herself.

She comes when no one else does. Midday isn't when people fetch water. But shame drives us into the heat if it means avoiding cold stares. Jesus asks her for a drink, shattering cultural lines. A Jewish man, a rabbi, alone with a Samaritan woman: this is scandal enough. Consider her history of fractured relationships, and this encounter becomes even more astonishing.

But Jesus knows. And he isn't repulsed. He doesn't moralize. He offers her water, which she didn't even know to request. "If you knew the gift of God . . . " He speaks of living water, of a well that won't run dry, of a thirst finally quenched not by hiding but by being seen.

She deflects at first, clings to practicalities, then retreats into theological debate. "Our ancestors worshiped on this mountain, but you Jews claim Jerusalem . . . " We often do this. When conviction gets close, we pivot to religion, to politics, to anything that keeps the gaze off our hearts.

But Jesus is relentless in love. He answers her question but redirects her to a deeper level. "A time is coming when true worshipers will worship the Father in spirit and truth." No longer bound by geography or ethnic division, worship becomes a matter of transformed hearts and unveiled lives.

He sees her completely. Names her reality. And still offers himself. This woman (nameless to us but known to God) becomes the first recorded evangelist in John's Gospel. She leaves her water jar, runs back into the village she had avoided, and cries out, "Come, see a man who told me everything I ever did. Could this be the Messiah?"

This story isn't just about her. It's about us. Our lives are filled with wells that never satisfy ambition, distraction, approval, and power. We come to them repeatedly, hoping to silence the ache. Jesus waits by these wells, not to shame us but to meet us. To offer water that becomes a spring inside us: grace welling up, washing over our shame, flooding our desert places.

For disciples, this means we must stop hiding. We bring our thirst and let Jesus name it. We abandon our old jars (the means we've used to numb ourselves) and run to tell others of the One who knows us fully and loves us still.

In a culture obsessed with surface, Jesus goes straight for the subterranean. He speaks to what lies beneath: the wounds, the desires, the longings. And invites us into worship that is honest and whole.

Guiding Truth: Jesus meets us in our thirst, not to condemn but to awaken, offering living water that transforms our worship and our witness.

Reflection: What wells am I still returning to that can't satisfy? Where might Jesus be asking me to worship in spirit and truth, without masks, without fear?

Prayer: Jesus, you who sit at my well, name my thirst. Give me water that lives. Dismantle my false securities and awaken true worship in me. May my story become an invitation for others to experience your grace. Amen.

Day 9: Harvest in Unexpected Fields

Reading: John 4:27–42

The disciples return, arms full of bread, only to find Jesus talking with a Samaritan woman. Their silence is loud: surprise, confusion, perhaps disapproval. A rabbi shouldn't be alone with her. But Jesus dismantles every social boundary with gentle disregard. His mission is bigger than their categories.

The woman leaves her jar. It's a small but profound symbol: she abandons the very vessel she came to fill. Running back to her village, she becomes the herald of grace, proclaiming, "Come, see a man who told me everything I ever did. Could this be the Messiah?" Her shame turns into testimony. Her story, once hidden, becomes the bridge by which others come to faith.

Meanwhile, the disciples urge Jesus to eat. They're consumed by the ordinary, by the immediate needs of stomachs and schedules. But Jesus has tasted something richer. "I have food to eat that you know nothing about." They miss the metaphor, stuck on the literal. How often we do the same, seeking daily bread yet blind to the feast of doing God's will.

Jesus then lifts their vision. "Open your eyes and look at the fields! They are ripe for harvest." This Samaritan village (outsiders, heretics in the eyes of Jerusalem) becomes holy ground. The harvest isn't waiting. It's already here, springing up in places they least expected.

And many believe, not because of theological arguments, but because of a woman's raw, imperfect witness. Her invitation to "Come and see" echoes through time. Her vulnerability breaks open curiosity. They come. They hear. They experience. And then their faith is born: "We no longer believe just because of what you said, now we have heard for ourselves."

For our spiritual lives, this passage reveals the movement of the gospel: how it flows through unlikely people, into unlikely places, and brings life where we've written off the soil as barren. It challenges our tribal instincts, our quiet prejudices, our tendency to think God only works within the lines we've drawn.

For disciples, it means leaving behind our jars (whatever we thought would satisfy) and running into the streets with stories of encounter. It means seeing mission not as a distant task but as a present reality. The fields are white. The harvest is now. Often in places, among people, and through means we didn't plan.

Jesus shows us that the kingdom grows through small testimonies, through risk and invitation, through hearts set ablaze by a love that knows us fully yet doesn't turn away.

Guiding Truth: God's harvest springs up in the most unexpected fields, inviting us to drop our jars and join the joyful work.

Reflection: What jar am I still clutching that Jesus is asking me to leave behind? Where might God be calling me to see harvest where I've only expected emptiness?

Prayer: Lord of the harvest, open my eyes to see your work around me. Help me let go of what I cling to and run with stories of your grace. Use even my imperfect witness to draw others into your life. Make me ready for fields I never imagined. Amen.

Day 10: Faith That Goes Beyond Signs

Reading: John 4:43–54

Jesus returns to Galilee, the land of his childhood, the soil that nurtured him as he grew. The people welcome him, but John's words carry a somber undertone: "They welcomed him, for they had seen all he had done in Jerusalem." They want wonders. They crave spectacle. It's easier to admire a miracle-worker than to surrender to a Lord.

Then comes a royal official. Desperation levels him. Titles and wealth mean little when a child lies dying. He pleads: "Come down before my child dies." It's a father's cry, stripped of pretense. And Jesus tests him with a sharp word: "Unless you people see signs and wonders, you will never believe." The rebuke isn't cruel, it's an invitation to deeper faith, to trust that runs beyond the need for proofs.

But the man persists. His plea isn't eloquent theology; it's raw, human need. "Sir, come down before my child dies." And here, mercy flows. Jesus replies, "Go, your son will live." No dramatic procession. No laying on of hands. Just a word sent forth like an arrow into the unknown.

The man takes Jesus at his word. He believes and turns homeward. Faith is often this quiet, trembling obedience: trust that walks before it sees. On the way, his servants meet him with news: the boy is alive. The fever broke at the very hour Jesus had spoken.

This is more than a healing story. It's a portrait of faith growing beyond signs. The official starts by wanting Jesus to come physically, to be present, to perform. But by the end, he believes simply in the word spoken. And not just him; his whole household comes to faith. A single act of trust ripples outward, altering the destiny of a family.

For our spiritual lives, this passage probes the nature of our own belief. Are we clinging to Jesus only when the signs are visible and the outcomes are assured? Or are we learning to walk home on nothing but his promise, hearts anchored in a word we have yet to see fulfilled?

It also speaks into how we live as disciples. We are surrounded by a culture that chases the spectacular: proofs, platforms, and public triumphs. But the kingdom often advances through unseen miracles, through trust that takes the next step without fanfare. Faith flourishes in quiet places, in hearts willing to take Jesus at his word and continue moving forward.

Jesus remains the One whose word holds life itself. He isn't bound by geography or immediacy. His power isn't limited to moments we can stage or control. The question becomes: will we trust him enough to walk the road home even when all we carry is his promise?

Guiding Truth: Genuine faith is born when we take Jesus at his word and walk forward before the evidence appears.

Reflection: Where am I waiting for signs instead of stepping out on trust? How might my quiet faith become a testimony that draws others into belief?

Prayer: Jesus, Word of Life, teach me to trust you even when I can't see. Strengthen me to walk in obedience on the thin edge of your promise. Let my faith become seed and shelter for others who long to believe. Amen.

Day 11: Do You Want to Be Made Well?

Reading: John 5:1–18

By the pool called Bethesda, a multitude of the unwell gather. Blind, lame, paralyzed: each hoping for a miracle stirred by angelic hands. It's a haunting picture: crowds of the desperate, all eyes fixed on troubled water, waiting for healing that may never come.

Jesus arrives and singles out one man who's been sick for thirty-eight years. Long enough for hope to scab over into resignation. Long enough to start building an identity around affliction. Jesus asks him a question that seems almost cruel in its simplicity: "Do you want to be made well?"

Not, "Do you believe, or will you try harder, or why haven't you figured this out by now?" Just: "Do you want this?" Desire is deeper than doctrine. Many of us cling to dysfunctions because they're familiar, predictable, and safer than change. Healing disrupts. It means stepping into an unknown future.

The man doesn't answer with a yes. Instead, he explains why it's impossible: "I have no one to help me . . . someone else always gets there first." His world is a story of scarcity—no one to carry him, no chance to win the race—a zero-sum spirituality.

But Jesus sidesteps the pool entirely. No angel, no water, no ritual. Just a command: "Get up! Pick up your mat and walk." Power surges not through sacred water, but through the Word made flesh. The man obeys, and suddenly, his muscles awaken, his limbs strengthen, and decades of paralysis unravel. He walks.

Yet immediately, controversy erupts. It's the Sabbath. The healed man carries his mat, breaking tradition. The religious leaders, guardians of order, care more about the breach of custom than the miracle of restoration. This is the scandal of grace: it doesn't fit institutional boxes. It disrupts systems built more on control than compassion.

Jesus later finds the man in the temple, no longer by the pool but in the place of worship. "See, you are well again. Stop sinning, or something worse may happen." This isn't a threat. It's a more profound healing. Physical restoration is only part of the salvation process. Wholeness touches body, soul, and story.

For our lives, this passage is a sharp summons. Where have we grown comfortable with our paralysis? What excuses keep us by stale waters, narrating our helplessness? Jesus still asks, "Do you want to be made well?" Healing often means letting go of self-pity, stepping beyond blame, and daring to move at his word.

As disciples, we must also recognize where rigid religion tries to police the work of God. Grace breaks rules that keep the suffering at bay. Mercy walks into our systems and tells paralyzed souls to rise. And the kingdom advances: one mat lifted, one healed heart at a time.

Guiding Truth: Jesus calls us out of resignation and into restoration, breaking old patterns with a living word that heals.

Reflection: Where am I still lying by the pool, explaining why transformation can't happen? How might Jesus be inviting me to rise, carry my story, and walk into new life?

Prayer: Christ, who speaks life into weary places, shatter my excuses. Lift me from familiar paralysis. Make me whole beyond what I imagine and let my very steps become testimony to your power and compassion. Amen.

Day 12: The Works of the Father

Reading: John 5:19–47

Jesus responds to accusations of Sabbath-breaking and blasphemy with words that are both gentle and thunderous. He doesn't defend himself with clever logic or social leverage. Instead, he roots everything in intimacy: "Very truly I tell you, the Son can do nothing by himself; he can do only what he sees the Father doing."

This isn't mere imitation. It's a union. A life so intertwined with God's heart that every act becomes a divine echo. The Father loves the Son and shows him all things. And so, the Son heals, raises, judges, gives life: each deed a mirror of the Father's compassion and justice.

These verses take us deeper still. Jesus speaks of a day when the dead will hear his voice and rise: some to life, others to judgment. The stakes are cosmic. He claims an authority that belongs only to God: to grant life, to execute judgment. And all so that the Son may be honored just as the Father is honored.

For us, this passage pierces through shallow discipleship. We often reduce following Jesus to moral improvement or doctrinal correctness. But here we see that to believe is to participate in divine life. To listen is to come alive. "Whoever hears my word and believes him who sent me has eternal life . . . and has crossed over from death to life." This isn't merely future hope but present reality: a new creation already unfurling.

Jesus also rebukes the religious leaders. They pore over the Scriptures, thinking knowledge itself will save them. Yet they refuse to come to him, the very Word the Scriptures testify about. It's a haunting warning for our study, preaching, and systems. We can be devoted to holy texts and still miss the living Christ standing right before us.

He exposes their hunger for human glory. They seek approval from one another rather than the honor that comes from God alone. True faith can't survive in the soil of reputation management. It flourishes only in the hidden ground of divine love.

And then Jesus brings Moses into the conversation. "If you believed Moses, you would believe me, for he wrote about me." The lawgiver points beyond himself. All sacred history bends toward Jesus. To reject him is to misunderstand the very Scriptures we claim to uphold.

For our lives, this passage is a summons to deeper union. To watch for what the Father is doing and let our days be shaped by that seeing. It calls us to trade approval for obedience, to hear the voice that raises dead places in us to life.

It's a call to let theology become encounter, study become surrender, and the radiant glory of Christ eclipse reputation.

Guiding Truth: True discipleship means laying down self-driven agendas to join in the life, love, and work of the Father revealed in Jesus.

Reflection: Where am I more concerned with approval from others than with the honor that comes from God? How can I slow down to watch and join what the Father is already doing around me?

Prayer: Living Word, draw me beyond mere knowledge into intimate trust. Let my life echo the compassion and justice of your heart. Silence my need for human applause and anchor me in the joy of your presence and purposes. Amen.

Day 13: The Bread That Breaks Open Trust

Reading: John 6:1–15

A vast crowd follows Jesus across the sea, hungry for signs, stirred by rumors of healing. They press in, thousands strong, carried by hope and desperation. Jesus looks at them with a shepherd's heart. But he also turns to test his disciples, asking Philip: "Where shall we buy bread for these people to eat?"

It's a question laced with impossibility. Philip does the math and comes up short. "It would take more than half a year's wages . . . " Scarcity speaks loudly in the minds of those trained by imperial economics. Andrew notices a boy with five barley loaves and two fish: hardly enough. Yet he offers it anyway, small and insufficient.

Jesus takes this meager gift, lifts it toward heaven, gives thanks, and begins to distribute. And wonder breaks loose. Bread multiplies. Fish fills empty hands. Thousands eat their fill on the slopes of Galilee. Scarcity gives way to abundance. Need is transformed by divine generosity.

But the story doesn't end with full stomachs. Jesus instructs the disciples, "Gather the pieces that are left over. Let nothing be wasted." Twelve baskets overflow. Grace is never stingy, yet always mindful. God's economy is abundance with reverence; enough to satisfy, enough to share, and enough to steward carefully.

Then the crowd moves in to make Jesus king by force. They want a leader who meets their needs on demand, a sovereign who secures bread lines and overthrows oppressors. But Jesus withdraws. He refuses to be reduced to their agenda. He came not merely to fill stomachs, but to draw hearts into trust that transcends transaction.

This passage speaks to our spiritual lives with haunting relevance. We live in cultures shaped by scarcity and fear. We clutch what we have, sure it'll never be enough. We measure our resources, our gifts, and our futures, and always come up short. Yet Jesus asks us to bring our small offerings anyway. He breaks and blesses what little we hold, turning poverty into provision.

But this miracle also confronts our temptation to make Jesus into a mascot for our projects. The crowd would crown him for his usefulness, not his lordship. We often seek Christ to secure our comfort and guarantee our plans. Yet he slips away from such grabs for power, calling us instead to trust, to follow, to feed others with the bread he multiplies.

As disciples, we are invited into this rhythm: to bring what we have, however inadequate; to watch it blessed and broken; to serve others from divine abundance; and to guard against turning Jesus into a mere provider of our preferences.

Guiding Truth: Jesus transforms our small offerings into overflowing grace, inviting trust beyond scarcity and agendas.

Reflection: Where am I holding back my small gifts out of fear that they aren't enough? How might I be trying to fit Jesus into my agenda rather than surrendering to his larger kingdom way?

Prayer: Generous Christ, take what little I hold (my hopes, my skills, my fragile trust) and bless it. Break it open for others. Guard me from shaping you into my image and teach me the freedom of simple trust. Feed many through these humble hands. Amen.

Day 14: Fear and the Voice Over the Waves

Reading: John 6:16–24

Evening settles on the lake. The disciples set out across dark water, leaving Jesus on the mountain. A storm gathers, wind howls, waves rise. They row, bone-tired, fighting against chaos that seems stronger than their skill. The sea in Scripture often symbolizes the untamed, the place where human power is exhausted, where we encounter the limits of our striving.

Then they see him: Jesus walking on the water, moving across the deep like the Spirit hovering over the primordial chaos. But their reaction isn't joy. It's terror. They mistake deliverance for a threat. We often do. When God comes close in ways that defy our categories, fear shouts louder than faith.

Jesus speaks into their storm with a simple, shattering declaration: "It's I; don't be afraid." The Greek echoes the divine name: "I AM." The same voice that spoke from the burning bush now speaks across the waves. The power that parts seas and stills creation walks toward them in human form.

John's gospel skips Peter's attempt to walk. The spotlight rests solely on Jesus's approach and the disciples' invitation. "Then they were willing to take him into the boat, and immediately the boat reached the shore where they were heading." The miracle here is layered. Christ steps into their fear, and suddenly, what was long and laborious resolves into safe arrival. Presence becomes deliverance.

For our spiritual lives, this passage meets us in all the places where storms rage: external circumstances that unravel us, internal anxieties that toss us around. We row hard against waves of uncertainty, loneliness, injustice, and loss. Often, we try to handle it alone, muscle through on our own power. Yet Jesus draws near precisely there, not with complicated answers but with his presence.

He comes in ways that unsettle us, walking over the very chaos we fear most, unbound by the limits we've accepted. And he speaks not first to fix the storm but to steady our hearts: "Do not be afraid."

This passage also calls us to a discipleship of trust that goes beyond control. The disciples couldn't calm the wind. They couldn't shorten the journey. All they could do was welcome Jesus into the boat. That was enough.

As followers of Christ, we're not promised tranquil seas. But we're promised the presence of One who treads upon the deep, who enters our fragile crafts, who carries us to shores we couldn't reach on our own. This is the heart of true security: not that life becomes stormless, but that God-with-us steps into our trembling boats.

Guiding Truth: Jesus meets us in the storm, inviting us to receive his presence over our fear, so we may arrive where striving alone could never take us.

Reflection: Where am I still rowing against the waves, afraid to welcome Jesus into my most vulnerable storms? What does it look like to trust his presence more than I fear the chaos around me?

Prayer: Lord who walks over my deepest fears, speak Your "I AM" into my storm. Silence my terror, enter my fragile boat, and bring me safely to your purpose. May your presence calm what my striving never could. Amen.

Day 15: The Bread That Offends and Satisfies

Reading: John 6:25–59

The crowds track Jesus down, chasing him across the sea. They want more bread. Their stomachs remember the miraculous feast on the hillside: five loaves, two fish, thousands fed. They pursue Jesus for another sign, another meal, another proof that God is useful.

Jesus exposes their hunger for what it is. "You're looking for me not because you saw the signs, but because you ate the loaves and had your fill." They long for a Messiah who fills their pantries, not their hearts. They crave security more than transformation.

Then Jesus speaks words that ignite the deepest ache: "Don't work for food that spoils, but for food that endures to eternal life." Their response is predictable: What must we do? Humanity always prefers earning to receiving. But Jesus dismantles the striving: "The work of God is this: to believe in the one he has sent." Trust, not toil, is the gateway to life.

Still, they demand another sign. "What will you do? Our ancestors ate manna in the wilderness . . . " Please give us a repeat of Moses. Jesus answers by drawing the line straight to himself: "I'm the bread of life." Not merely a supplier of bread: the bread. True satisfaction isn't in what he gives, but in who he is.

This offends them. It always does. They grumble. They remember his family, his hometown, this ordinary carpenter's son. How can he claim to be bread that comes down from heaven? Jesus doesn't soften it. He presses further, speaks of eating his flesh and drinking his blood. It's scandalous, almost grotesque. Yet underneath it lies the most tremendous promise: union. To consume him is to receive life itself. To abide in him is to share in the very vitality of God.

For our spiritual lives, this passage tears through the superficial ways we use God. We want Jesus to bless our agendas, to fill our lack, to keep life manageable. But he offers something infinitely greater and more demanding. He offers himself. He becomes our nourishment, our center, our very life.

This means discipleship isn't about adding spiritual accessories to bolster an otherwise self-sufficient existence. It's about feeding on Christ daily: letting his words, his heart, his way seep into our bones. It's about trusting that only he can satisfy the deep hungers that applause, ambition, consumption, and even religion can never fill.

It also means accepting a way that offends our sense of what is right and wrong. The cross is foolishness. Eating his flesh, drinking his blood: these are stumbling blocks to pride. But in embracing them, we find the food that truly endures.

Guiding Truth: Jesus doesn't come to give us bread but to be our bread: our only true satisfaction, our life beyond every lesser hunger.

Reflection: Where am I still chasing Jesus for what he can give me rather than for who he is? What would it look like today to feast on Christ alone as my deepest sustenance?

Prayer: Bread of Life, feed my soul with yourself. Wean me off the shallow satisfactions that leave me empty. Let your life become my life, your strength my sustenance. Draw me into deeper union with you, where my deepest hungers are met. Amen.

Day 16: The Offense and the Clinging

Reading: John 6:60–71

Many of Jesus's disciples now murmur. "This is a hard teaching. Who can accept it?" The words of eating his flesh and drinking his blood, of him being the sole bread of life, scrape against their sensibilities. It's too raw, too strange, too costly. They had followed Jesus for miracles, for power, for hopes of liberation. But now he asks for something more profound: trust beyond understanding, union that costs them the right to keep him at a distance.

Jesus, knowing their hearts, doesn't chase after them with soft reassurances. Instead, he presses harder. "Does this offend you? Then what if you see the Son of Man ascend to where he was before!" If they stumble over bread imagery, how will they face the scandal of a crucified Messiah ascending in resurrection glory? Flesh profits nothing, he says; it's the Spirit who gives life. His words aren't for casual ears: they are Spirit and life, and only those drawn by the Father can truly hear.

Then many turn back. They leave. The crowd thins, revealing the shallow nature of their allegiance. This is one of the most haunting moments in the Gospels: disciples abandoning the Way because it's not the way they imagined.

Jesus looks at the Twelve. His question is heartbreakingly vulnerable: "You don't want to leave, too, do you?" This is God standing open-hearted before fragile humans, asking if they'll stay.

Peter answers for them all and perhaps for us in our best moments. "Lord, to whom shall we go? You have the words of eternal life. We have come to believe and know that you are the Holy One of God." It's not that Peter understands. It's that there is nowhere else to turn. The life he longs for lives in Jesus alone.

But even here, shadows linger. Jesus says, "Have I not chosen you, the Twelve? Yet one of you is a devil." Judas stands among the faithful, outwardly close yet inwardly drifting toward betrayal. It's possible to walk beside Christ, hear his words, perform the motions of discipleship, and still hold a heart that turns away.

This passage strikes a deep chord in our modern spiritual lives. We are often tempted to follow Jesus only when his way is convenient, when it aligns with our preferences, our politics, our prosperity. But Jesus refuses to be a mascot for our agendas. His teaching wounds before it heals, disrupts before it comforts. The call is to feed on him alone, to stake everything on his sufficiency, even when much remains unclear.

True discipleship means clinging when others walk away. It means confessing with Peter: There is no one else. You alone have life.

Guiding Truth: When Jesus's words are hardest, true faith stays not because it fully understands, but because it knows there is nowhere else to find life.

Reflection: Where am I tempted to walk away when Jesus's teaching cuts against my desires or cultural comforts? How can I more deeply root my life in the confession that only Christ holds eternal life?

Prayer: Holy One, when your words unsettle me, anchor me still. Keep me from turning back when the road narrows. Help me confess, even through confusion, that you alone have life. Hold me close when faith feels thin and keep me clinging to you. Amen.

Day 17: Hiddenness and Holy Boldness

Reading: John 7:1–24

The tension is rising. Religious leaders seek Jesus's life, watching for a misstep that might justify their violence. His brothers prod him to show himself, urging a spectacle. "Leave Galilee and go to Judea . . . so that your disciples may see the works you do." They want him to seize the stage, to prove himself with public wonders. They don't yet believe, though they cloak their taunts in strategy.

But Jesus moves differently. "My time isn't yet here." There is a divine timetable at work, not manipulated by human agendas or driven by fame. Jesus goes to the festival in secret, refusing to bow to demands for applause or quick validation. In hiddenness, he honors the Father's will.

Midway through the feast, Jesus begins teaching openly. The crowds marvel. "How did this man get such learning without having been taught?" Their categories fracture. Wisdom that transcends formal schooling pours from the carpenter's son. Jesus clarifies: "My teaching isn't my own. It comes from the One who sent Me." True authority is never self-made. It flows from communion with God, not credentials.

Then he slices into their hypocrisy. They rage at him for healing on the Sabbath yet circumcise on the Sabbath to keep tradition. "Stop judging by mere appearances," he says, "but instead judge correctly." This is a call that echoes still: to discern truth not by shallow optics, not by surface loyalties, but by the deeper heart of God's justice and mercy.

For our spiritual lives, this passage confronts our addiction to spectacle. Like Jesus's brothers, we want quick revelation, swift vindication, and proofs that satisfy our craving for certainty. But Jesus moves by a slower wisdom. Often, the holiest work is hidden, misunderstood, unfolding on divine rather than cultural schedules.

It also speaks to how we discern truth in an age obsessed with image. We are quick to judge by appearances: by charisma, crowds, aesthetics, tribal alignment. But Jesus calls us deeper. "Judge correctly." This means weighing lives and teachings by the fruits of compassion, humility, righteousness, and love, not by performance.

As disciples, we're invited to embrace both the hiddenness and the boldness of Jesus. To walk quietly when God says wait, to speak truth even when it invites scorn, to rest our authority not on clever arguments or institutional power but on being sent, rooted in intimacy with the Father.

This isn't the way of quick influence. It's the slow work of becoming so aligned with God that our words and lives carry heaven's weight, regardless of earthly applause.

Guiding Truth: Christ teaches us to resist shallow judgments and to move by divine timing: hidden, when necessary, boldly truthful when called.

Reflection: Where am I tempted to demand spectacle from God instead of trusting the hidden, unfolding work? How can I learn to judge rightly, looking beyond appearances to what reveals God's justice and mercy?

Prayer: Jesus, gentle and fearless, teach me to wait when you wait and speak when you speak. Strip me of surface judgments and root me in discernment that mirrors your heart. Make me content with hidden obedience and courageous in truth. Amen.

Day 18: Thirst and Division

Reading: John 7:25–52

Jerusalem is electric with rumor. Some say Jesus is the Messiah; others dismiss him for coming from Galilee. "When the Messiah comes, no one will know where he is from." They think they understand how God works: mystery must look a certain way. Jesus upends their expectations, declaring boldly in the temple courts, "You know me, and you know where I'm from. I have not come on my own."

His origin is deeper than Nazareth, older than time. He comes sent by God, not self-appointed. But his words only deepen the divide. Some try to seize him, yet no hand can close around him: his hour has not yet come. Even the opposition bends to divine sovereignty.

Then, on the last and greatest day of the festival, Jesus stands and cries out: "Let anyone who is thirsty come to me and drink. Whoever believes in me, as Scripture has said, rivers of living water will flow from within them." It's an audacious claim. In a city fixated on ritual purification, Jesus positions himself as the new fountain of life. Not stagnant pools, but flowing rivers. Not contained by temple courts but gushing from within every believer by the Spirit.

This is the promise that transcends ritual: God's life pouring through human vessels. Yet even this invitation ignites controversy. Some declare, "Surely this man is the Prophet." Others insist, "He is the Messiah." Still others object: "The Messiah doesn't come from Galilee." They clutch familiar interpretations, blind to the living revelation before them.

Meanwhile, the temple guards return empty-handed. Sent to arrest Jesus, they return instead awed: "No one ever spoke the way this man does." The religious leaders sneer, sure that only the unlearned believe. Nicodemus tentatively speaks up, reminding them of justice, but his cautious defense is mocked.

This passage cuts painfully close to our religious habits. How often do we judge others by their credentials, background, or theological affiliations, missing the living Christ who stands before us? How easily we divide over interpretations, doctrines, tribal affiliations: clutching tight to being right, even as living water flows elsewhere.

For our spiritual lives, Jesus's call is piercing. "If you are thirsty, come to Me." Not to systems, not to the security of being correct, but to him. Our divisions often reveal not our zeal for truth, but our fear of surrender. Drinking from Christ means letting him define life, uprooting certainty, and turning us into channels of grace that we can't control.

As disciples, we are invited to resist shallow judgments, to stop securing our boundaries so fiercely, and to open our hearts to the Spirit who flows wherever God pleases. The rivers Christ promises aren't tame. They carve new paths, flood familiar ground, heal lands long parched.

Guiding Truth: Jesus invites our thirsty souls to himself, offering living water that defies our categories and flows beyond our control.

Reflection: Where am I clinging to old certainties or boundaries that keep me from truly coming to Jesus? What might change if I let his Spirit flow through me like rivers, uncontained and free?

Prayer: Fountain of life, break open my rigid places. Let your living water rush through my fears and undo my boundaries. Quench my thirst with nothing less than yourself and make me a vessel that overflows with your Spirit. Amen.

Day 19: Stones Dropped, Mercy Written

Reading: John 7:53–8:11

At dawn, Jesus sits in the temple courts, teaching. People press close, hungry for words that cut deeper and heal truer than any they've known. Suddenly, the quiet breaks: religious leaders shove forward a woman, disheveled, terrified. Caught in adultery. Her sin is public, her shame weaponized. They care nothing for her soul. She is bait, a pawn to trap Jesus.

"Moses commanded us to stone such women. Now what do you say?" If Jesus sides with the law, he betrays his mercy. If he dismisses it, he discredits the law itself. Either way, they believe they have him cornered.

But Jesus stoops. He writes on the ground. The text doesn't tell us what he inscribes. Perhaps it's a mystery meant to search us. He lets silence stretch until accusation becomes its indictment. Then he stands and speaks words that unravel every clenched hand: "Let any one of you who is without sin be the first to throw a stone."

Conviction ripples through the crowd. Stones slip from fingers. Accusers depart, oldest first: those who have lived long enough to know the weight of their failures.

Now only Jesus and the woman remain. Holiness and brokenness face to face. She waits for condemnation. Instead, she hears astonishing mercy: "Neither do I condemn you. Go now and leave your life of sin."

This isn't soft permissiveness. Jesus neither minimizes her sin nor exalts it into identity. He names it and then offers her a future unshackled by it. Grace that doesn't ignore sin but frees from its power. Mercy that says, "You aren't the sum of your worst choices." Now walk differently.

For our spiritual lives, this passage speaks volumes. We live in cultures of stones: social media mobs, religious tribunals, self-righteous judgments. We are quick to label, to shame, to secure our goodness by exposing someone else's guilt. Yet Jesus stoops. Writes. Waits. Confronts our need to condemn with a mirror held up to our souls.

As disciples, we're called to drop our stones. To recognize that we stand on level ground with every sinner we'd like to sentence. To embrace a grace that stuns us first, then changes how we see others. We're also called to hear his voice to us personally, naming our brokenness, yet sending us forth unchained, forgiven, and commissioned to a new way.

This is how the kingdom advances: not by securing our moral superiority, but by embodying the mercy of Christ that writes stories of redemption in dust.

Guiding Truth: Jesus meets us in our shame, not with stones but with mercy, calling us to walk free and offer that same mercy to others.

Reflection: Where am I still clutching stones of judgment, against others or myself? How is Jesus inviting me to leave old patterns and walk in the newness of grace?

Prayer: Merciful Christ, unclench my fists. Let the stones of my condemnation fall. Speak your freeing words over my life and teach me to walk and to love as one forgiven. May my story be dust inscribed with your grace. Amen.

Day 20: Light for Those Who Will Follow

Reading: John 8:12–30

Jesus stands in the temple courts and declares, "I'm the light of the world. Whoever follows me will never walk in darkness but will have the light of life." This is more than a poetic metaphor. It's an audacious claim, standing in the place where massive lamps were lit during the Feast of Tabernacles to recall the pillar of fire that guided Israel through the wilderness. Jesus claims to be that very guiding light, God's presence leading lost humanity home.

The Pharisees push back. They demand legal proof, external validation. "Here you are, appearing as your witness; your testimony isn't valid." But Jesus isn't bound by human courtroom rules. "My testimony is valid, for I know where I came from and where I'm going." They judge by shallow appearances. He sees into eternity.

Jesus exposes their spiritual blindness. "You don't know me or my Father. If you knew me, you would know my Father also." They cling to religious heritage but miss the very One all their traditions point toward. Their hearts remain veiled, content with ritual when a relationship stands before them.

This isn't a tame conversation. Jesus insists: "If you don't believe that I'm he, you will indeed die in your sins." It sounds harsh in our gentle ears, but it's the urgency of love. Light has come. To reject it is to choose stumbling in darkness forever.

Still, they press him: "Who are you?" Jesus points them again to his union with the Father. "When you have lifted the Son of Man, then you will know that I'm he." The cross, the ultimate lifting up, will become the final unveiling: where divine love and justice meet, where light shines most brilliantly through wounded flesh.

As he speaks, many believe. His words break through intellectual arguments and pierce hearts longing for more than law, more than ritual, more than empty certainty.

For our spiritual lives, this passage demands that we face our darkness. We all have corners of secrecy, shadows we tolerate, places we'd rather not let light touch. Jesus doesn't simply offer advice or inspiration. He offers himself: light that uncovers but also heals, illuminates but also guides.

Following Jesus means leaving the comfortable dark. It means letting his brilliance expose illusions, reveal hidden idols, and dismantle our carefully constructed self-deceptions. Yet only there, in that raw honesty, do we truly see. Only then do we walk in the light of life.

As disciples in a world flooded with artificial lights (distractions, ideologies, quick fixes), Jesus still stands in our midst and declares, "I'm the light." Not one more option among many, but the very radiance of God drawing us out of the shadow into the vast expanse of grace.

Guiding Truth: Jesus isn't merely a light guide: he is the light, calling us to leave our shadows and live fully in him.

Reflection: What places in my life am I still trying to keep hidden from the searching brilliance of Christ? How might following Jesus into the light transform my perspective on myself, others, and the world?

Prayer: Light of the world, shine on my hidden places. Chase away my shadows. Lead me out of darkness and teach me to walk in the brightness of your truth and love. Please make me a bearer of your light to others lost in shadow. Amen.

Day 21: Before Abraham Was, I AM

Reading: John 8:31–59

This long, tense dialogue stretches from hopeful belief to bitter resistance. Jesus begins by inviting would-be disciples into true freedom: "If you hold to my teaching, you are my disciples. Then you will know the truth, and the truth will set you free."

They bristle, clutching their lineage. "We are Abraham's descendants . . . never been slaves!" Ignorant of Rome's shadow, and even more naive to sin's deeper chains. Jesus speaks past their defenses: "Everyone who sins is a slave to sin." Freedom isn't inherited. It's received from the Son, who alone breaks the bondage of self and shadow.

Their protests escalate. They cling to Abraham, to history, to sacred identity. Jesus insists that true kinship with Abraham means echoing his faith: hearing God's voice, yielding in trust. But these leaders plot murder. They resemble not Abraham, but another father: one who spins lies and resists the truth. "You belong to your father, the devil," Jesus declares, unmasking the spiritual allegiance beneath the religious façade.

The confrontation turns sharper. They call Jesus a Samaritan and demon-possessed. He stands unflinching. "I honor my Father . . . I don't seek my glory." His words are laced with promise even amid the tension: "Whoever obeys my word will never see death."

Now they erupt: "Are you greater than our father Abraham? Who do you think you are?" Jesus responds with staggering clarity, pulling the veil off eternity: "Before Abraham was born, I AM." Not merely older. Eternal. Not just a teacher of truth. Truth itself, divine existence unveiled. The name spoken from the burning bush now stands clothed in flesh before them.

They pick up stones. Their religious zeal, stripped of humility, turns murderous. But Jesus slips away. His hour has not yet come. Divine timing governs even the fury of misguided piety.

For our spiritual lives, this passage lays bare two paths. One clings to status, history, and self-deception, boasting of spiritual pedigree while nursing rebellion. The other hears Jesus's hard, liberating truth and stays, abiding in His word, discovering freedom, and entering life.

We must ask: Do we love truth enough to let it expose us? Are we willing to find our deepest identity not in ancestry, tradition, or personal mythologies, but in Christ alone? This passage reminds us that discipleship means letting Jesus rewrite our story, overriding every lesser claim on who we are.

It also means bowing before mystery. "Before Abraham was, I AM." Here, eternity breaches time, and we are left to either harden or worship. The One who stands before us is no mere moral guide. He is the living God, inviting us to drop our stones, abandon our illusions, and find real life in him.

Guiding Truth: True freedom and identity are found only in abiding in Christ's word, trusting the One who isn't just older than Abraham but the eternal I AM.

Reflection: Where am I still resisting Jesus's truth because it threatens my illusions or comforts? How might surrendering my identity to the great I AM reshape my freedom, my story, my hope?

Prayer: Eternal Christ, I lay down every false claim to identity and freedom. Speak your truth into my deep places, even when it wounds. Make me a true child of your promise, rooted in your Word, shaped by your love, alive in your life. Amen.

Day 22: Mud, Spit, and Sight

Reading: John 9:1–12

Jesus and his disciples pass a man who is blind from birth. The disciples reduce his pain to a theological puzzle: "Rabbi, who sinned, this man or his parents, that he was born blind?" It's easier to theorize about suffering than to stand alongside it. Easier to blame than to bless.

But Jesus dismantles their assumptions. "Neither this man nor his parents sinned . . . but this happened so that the works of God might be displayed in him." This doesn't mean God delights in affliction. It means God enters our broken stories, reworking them into places of revelation and transformation. Suffering becomes soil where grace roots and grows.

Jesus then does something profoundly human and deeply divine. He spits on the ground, makes mud, and smears it on the man's eyes. Dust and breath; echoes of Eden. Creation mingled with saliva, a new genesis forming. "Go," he says, "wash in the Pool of Siloam." The man obeys, stumbles to water still blind, washes, and emerges seeing. Light floods places long resigned to darkness.

Neighbors are astonished, confused. "Isn't this the same man who used to sit and beg?" Some say yes. Others deny it. Transformation always disrupts familiar categories. The healed man answers simply: "I'm the man." Once identified by blindness, he now bears witness to grace.

This story presses on our spiritual lives with uncomfortable power. We often echo the disciples' logic, trying to explain pain by tracing blame. We look for sin behind misfortune, cause behind tragedy: an attempt to keep chaos at bay. But Jesus redirects our vision. The deeper question isn't, "Who's at fault?" But "How might God reveal mercy here?"

Discipleship means standing near suffering without neat explanations. It means believing that even our deepest darkness can become a stage for God's luminous work. Sometimes Jesus heals with a word. Sometimes with mud and spit, processes that feel messy, even humiliating. He always calls us to respond, to trust, to wash where he sends us, even before we see.

This passage also invites us to examine how we respond to others' transformations. Like the neighbors, we may struggle to recognize people once confined by labels or pasts. Grace challenges our memory. Who are they if not blind beggars? Who are we if not the ones who knew their story first?

Jesus still smears mud, still sends people to wash, still brings sight where resignation once ruled. The question is whether we will join in wonder or retreat into cynicism.

Guiding Truth: Jesus enters our darkest places, reshaping pain into revelation, and calls us to trust his strange ways of healing.

Reflection: Where am I reducing suffering to blame instead of asking how God might reveal grace? What muddy places might Jesus be inviting me to trust, letting him work through, means I don't fully understand?

Prayer: Healing Christ, touch my blindness with your living hands. Use even mud and spit if you must. Teach me to trust your ways beyond my logic, and let my life become a witness that says, "I'm the one you healed." Amen.

Day 23: Eyes Opened, Hearts Exposed

Reading: John 9:13–41

The healed man is brought before the Pharisees. A miracle has occurred: a man blind from birth now sees. You would expect a celebration. Instead, there's interrogation. Because Jesus healed on the Sabbath, this joy becomes a case file, a threat to rigid systems more committed to rule-keeping than to restoration.

The Pharisees press him: "How did he open your eyes?" The man recounts it. They probe again. Some accuse Jesus outright. Others wonder if God might truly be at work. But institutional fear resists wonder.

They call the man's parents. Terrified of excommunication, they dodge responsibility: "He is of age; ask him." Religion that uses fear to maintain control always silences the vulnerable and isolates the healed.

So again, they summon the man. They demand conformity: "Give glory to God by telling the truth. We know this man is a sinner." But he stands on his lived encounter: "Whether he is a sinner or not, I don't know. One thing I do know: I was blind but now I see." Testimony rooted in transformation cuts through theological posturing.

Frustrated, they try to trap him in contradiction. Instead, his courage sharpens: "Do you want to become his disciples too?" They mock him, hurl insults, and insist they are Moses' disciples. Yet ironically, it's they who stand unable to see the God who stands before them, healing, loving, subverting their tidy boxes.

They throw the man out. This is what rigid religion does when confronted with uncontrollable grace: it exiles those who refuse to deny their encounter.

Then Jesus finds him. Always seeking the outcast. "Do you believe in the Son of Man?" The man, cast out by the temple, is welcomed by God in the flesh. "Lord, I believe," he says, and worships.

Jesus concludes with words that still thunder: "For judgment I have come into this world, so that the blind will see and those who see will become blind." The Pharisees bristle: "Are we blind too?" Jesus replies, "If you were blind, you wouldn't be guilty of sin; but now that you claim you can see, your guilt remains."

For our spiritual lives, this passage exposes how easily we substitute systems for intimacy, certainty for compassion, and control for the wild work of grace. Actual discipleship risks confessing ignorance to see anew. It stands vulnerable before mystery, willing to say, "I only know this: once I was blind, now I see."

It also warns us that spiritual pride is the darkest blindness. Those most certain of their vision may miss God entirely, present in humble acts, disruptive healings, Sabbath-breaking compassion.

As disciples, we are called to live in humble sight, testifying not to how much we know, but to how deeply we've been changed.

Guiding Truth: Christ comes to give sight to those who admit blindness and to humble those who cling to false certainty.

Reflection: Where have I become so sure of my spiritual sight that I can no longer see Jesus working beyond my categories? How can I better testify, simply and humbly, to the grace that has opened my eyes?

Prayer: Jesus, Light of the World, keep me from the blindness of pride. Make me quick to confess, eager to learn, ready to marvel. Let my life proclaim repeatedly, "I was ignorant and deceived, but now I see." Amen.

Day 24: The Voice of the Shepherd

Reading: John 10:1–21

Jesus paints images of sheep, gates, thieves, and shepherds to reveal the tender ferocity of God's care. The people still reeling from the healing of the man born blind (and the religious leaders' harsh response) now hear Jesus name himself the True Shepherd.

"Anyone who doesn't enter the sheep pen by the gate, but climbs in some other way, is a thief and a robber." It's a searing judgment. Many individuals ascend to positions of spiritual authority through power, manipulation, and fear. They don't love the sheep; they devour them. But the Shepherd enters rightly. The gatekeeper knows him. His voice calls by name, and the sheep recognize the one who has always known them.

Then Jesus deepens the mystery. "I'm the gate." He's not just the leader at the front; he is the way in. Safety, sustenance, life: they all flow through him. "Whoever enters through me will be saved. They'll come in and go out and find pasture."

Contrast fills his words: "The thief comes only to steal and kill and destroy; I have come that they may have life and have it to the full." The kingdom Jesus brings isn't mere survival. It's abundance, wholeness, life overflowing beyond scarcity's bleak lines.

Then the most staggering claim: "I'm the good Shepherd. The good Shepherd lays down his life for the sheep." Leaders preserve themselves; Jesus pours himself out. Hirelings run when wolves come, Jesus stays, fights, and bleeds. This Shepherd loves unto death.

He goes on: "I know my sheep and my sheep know me; just as the Father knows me and I know the Father." Our belonging to Christ is woven into the intimacy of the Trinity itself. We aren't anonymous followers; we are named, known, and folded into divine communion.

Jesus also breaks every boundary of insider religion: "I have other sheep that aren't of this sheep pen. I must bring them also." His heart aches for every flock we've labeled "other." One flock, one Shepherd: this is the future he labors toward, beyond our small sects and sharp divisions.

But even here, division rises. Some say Jesus is demon-possessed. Others marvel. The light of Christ always exposes. Hearts reveal themselves when confronted with a Shepherd who dies for his sheep.

For our lives, this passage calls us to recognize competing voices (many clamor for our loyalty): voices of fear, performance, consumerism, and tribal pride. The thief's work is subtle, beckoning us to graze on poisoned ground. Only one voice leads to an abundant life.

As disciples, we learn to listen for the tone of love, to discern it in prayer, Scripture, community, and silence. To trust that the Shepherd who calls us by name also guards us, provides for us, and will walk every valley with us, even death's shadow.

Guiding Truth: Jesus is both our gate and our Shepherd, calling us by name into a life of fearless abundance and sacrificial belonging.

Reflection: Which voices in my life steal joy and lead me away from the Shepherd's call? How is Jesus inviting me to trust his care more deeply and follow where he leads, beyond my safe fences?

Prayer: Good Shepherd, call my name again. Tune my ears to your voice above all counterfeit guides. Lead me into your life that overflows, and teach me to follow you with trust, even where the path grows dark. Hold me close. Amen.

Day 25: Held in the Hand of God

Reading: John 10:22–42

It's winter in Jerusalem, and Jesus walks in Solomon's Colonnade. The religious leaders surround him; their questions are edged with accusation. "How long will you keep us in suspense? If you are the Messiah, tell us." But their demand for plain speech is hollow. They have seen his works (healing, feeding, and restoring sight), yet they still refuse to believe.

Jesus answers with tender, devastating clarity: "I did tell you, but you don't believe. The works I do in my Father's name testify about me, but you don't believe because you aren't my sheep." It isn't ignorance that blinds them, but hardened hearts that won't recognize the Shepherd's voice.

Then Jesus opens a window into the deepest assurance a disciple can hold: "My sheep listen to my voice; I know them, and they follow me. I give them eternal life, and they shall never perish; no one will snatch them out of my hand." He goes further still. "My Father, who has given them to me, is greater than all; no one can snatch them out of my Father's hand. I and the Father are one."

We are doubly held, grasped by the Son's strong hand and secured by the Father's unassailable grasp. This isn't a fragile belonging. It's covenant love that locks eternity around fragile souls.

The leaders pick up stones. Unity with the Father is blasphemy in their ears. They refuse to see that the One before them embodies all the goodness, justice, mercy, and holiness they claim to defend. Jesus answers with Scripture and reason, inviting them again to believe based on the works themselves. But hearts chained to self-righteousness rarely loosen under logic. Instead of worship, they plot to seize him. Yet he slips away: his hour is still held in divine timing.

This passage digs deep into our spiritual lives. We, too, are prone to demand proofs from God on our terms, as if more evidence would override a heart that prefers its sovereignty. We want Jesus to conform to expectations, to speak plainly in ways that require no costly trust.

Yet discipleship is always about hearing the Shepherd's voice (through Scripture, prayer, and the Spirit's gentle tug) and following where it leads. It means resting in the astonishing promise: we are known, loved, and given eternal life. Hands hold us no power can pry open, not even our trembling failures.

This truth also shapes our lives. It roots out fear, because no thief can snatch us away. It uproots pride, because we did not climb into this safety ourselves; we were given. And it invites us to stand secure even amid hostility, knowing that Christ's sheep are never abandoned, no matter how dark the valley.

Guiding Truth: Jesus and the Father together hold us with unbreakable hands, inviting us to live fearlessly and respond to the Shepherd's voice.

Reflection: Where am I still demanding Jesus prove himself on my terms instead of trusting his works and words? How might knowing I'm doubly held by the Son and the Father free me from fear today?

Prayer: Strong Shepherd, steady my heart in your grasp. Let me rest in hands that never fail. Teach me to hear your voice above my doubts and to follow you with courage, held fast by love that will never let me go. Amen.

Day 26: The Weeping God and the Grave Unsealed

Reading: John 11:1–44

Word comes to Jesus: "Lord, the one you love is sick." Lazarus, friend and brother to Mary and Martha, lies dying in Bethany. Strangely, Jesus doesn't rush. He remains two days longer, speaking a paradox: "This sickness won't end in death." Yet Lazarus dies. Sometimes love allows delay, letting a deeper glory unfold that our urgent hearts can't yet fathom.

When Jesus finally arrives, Martha goes out to meet him, grief sharpening her words: "Lord, if you had been here, my brother wouldn't have died." Beneath her statement lies a wound we all know: Where were you? Why didn't you come sooner?

Jesus responds with revelation: "Your brother will rise again." Martha clings to future theology: "I know he'll rise at the resurrection on the last day." But Jesus draws resurrection from the distant horizon into the present: "I'm the resurrection and the life." Not merely a promise for someday, but a person here and now, life himself standing amid tombstones.

Mary comes next, falls at his feet, and echoes Martha's lament. Jesus sees her weeping, sees the gathered mourners, and is deeply moved. The Greek quivers with anguish and outrage. Then comes the shortest, rawest sentence in Scripture: "Jesus wept." God's tears mingle with human sorrow. The maker of life stands at death's door and sobs.

They led him to the tomb. A stone seals the darkness. Jesus commands: "Take away the stone." Martha protests, "Lord, by this time, there is a bad odor." We all fear what resurrection might expose. But Jesus presses beyond dignity and decay: "Did I not tell you that if you believe, you will see the glory of God?"

They roll away the stone. Jesus prays not for his own sake, but so that they might believe. Then, with a voice that pierced creation's first darkness, he calls: "Lazarus, come out!" And life erupts from death. The dead man shuffles forth, grave clothes clinging like old lies. "Unbind him and let him go." This is resurrection: God's voice summoning us from rot and wrapping, commanding us into liberty.

For our lives, this passage names both comfort and challenge. Jesus doesn't stand aloof from our grief; he weeps. He knows our delays, our confusion, our anguished "if onlys." Yet he also insists on rolling stones away, calling us into places that smell of disappointment and loss, daring to speak life where all we've prepared for is mourning.

Discipleship means trusting him to stand before our sealed tombs and believing he can still call forth something living. It means letting him undo our funeral wrappings, freeing us into a startling newness.

Guiding Truth: Jesus meets us in our grief with tears and stands at our tombs to call us out into a life of resurrection.

Reflection: Where have I sealed off hope, convinced the story is over? How might Jesus be asking me to trust him to roll away stones I've accepted as permanent?

Prayer: Resurrecting Christ, stand before my tombs. Speak life where I've surrendered to death. Unbind my heart from old graves and teach me to walk in the freedom of your voice, alive again by grace. Amen.

Day 27: Plotting Death Against Life

Reading: John 11:45–57

Word of Lazarus's resurrection spreads like wildfire. Many who see the dead man walking come to believe in Jesus. Life can't help but testify. But light always provokes darkness. The chief priests and Pharisees gather, disturbed not by evil but by power they can't control. "What are we accomplishing? Here is this man performing many signs. If we let him go on like this, everyone will believe in him, and then the Romans will come and take away both our temple and our nation."

Their fear is revealing. They are more concerned about preserving position and privilege than welcoming the very Messiah their Scriptures promised. Better to cling to fragile security than risk surrender to a kingdom that might upend their structures.

Then Caiaphas, the high priest, speaks words meant in cold calculation but caught up into divine prophecy: "It's better for you that one man die for the people than that the whole nation perish." Without knowing, he echoes eternity's plan: Jesus will indeed die for the people, but not to preserve old power. His death will break chains far deeper than Roman occupation; it'll unravel the reign of sin and death itself.

So, from that day, they plotted to kill him. Their hearts lock around violence, convinced that eliminating Jesus will save their way of life. Ironically, in striving to preserve the temple and nation, they miss the living temple who stood among them, offering a new covenant that would embrace every tribe and tongue.

Jesus withdraws to the wilderness near Ephraim, a quiet place with his disciples. Even now, timing belongs to the Father. The Passover nears. Pilgrims wonder if Jesus will come to the festival. The leaders stand ready, having given orders that anyone who knows his whereabouts should report him. Death stalks the edges of this story; unaware it's being lured into its defeat.

For our spiritual lives, this passage lays bare how fear of losing power, comfort, or certainty can harden into murderous resolve. We may not plot crucifixions, but we often resist any transformation that might cost us our illusions of control. We silence prophets, dismiss miracles, and tighten our grip on systems that serve us.

It also shows us that God's redemptive purposes often move right through human schemes. Caiaphas intends to secure national stability through one death; God wants to save the cosmos through the Lamb who takes away the world's sin. The cross will be history's cruelest injustice and heaven's most incredible mercy.

As disciples, we are called to trust a kingdom that often confounds earthly logic. To lay down our fragile securities and let Jesus disrupt what needs undoing, even when it feels like everything might collapse. Because sometimes resurrection requires that old structures die.

Guiding Truth: God's purposes prevail even through human plots, inviting us to surrender our fragile securities to the deeper story of redemption.

Reflection: Where am I clinging to power or comfort that resists Jesus's unsettling grace? How might trusting God's larger story free me to embrace costly transformation?

Prayer: Sovereign Christ, expose where I hold tight to my kingdoms. Loosen my grip. Let your death dismantle my lesser securities, and your resurrection lead me into new, daring trust. Write your larger story through my surrendered life. Amen.

Day 28: Fragrance That Fills the House

Reading: John 12:1–11

Six days before Passover, Jesus returns to Bethany. It's a tender scene: back to the village of resurrection, to the friends who welcomed him when others plotted his death. Lazarus reclines at the table, a living testament to the fact that Jesus holds power over death and the grave. Martha serves, moving in love's familiar rhythm.

Then Mary does something so raw, so lavish, it shatters all sense of propriety. She breaks open a jar of pure nard (worth a year's wages) and pours it over Jesus's feet. The fragrance explodes into every corner. She wipes his feet with her hair; a gesture so intimate it unsettles the room.

Judas objects, cloaking greed in the language of compassion. "Why wasn't this perfume sold and the money given to the poor?" He doesn't care for people experiencing poverty; he cares for his purse. But Jesus sees Mary's act for what it is: prophetic, priestly, preparing his body for burial before the cross makes sense to anyone.

"Leave her alone," Jesus says. "It was intended that she should save this perfume for the day of my burial. You will always have the poor among you, but you won't always have me." It isn't a dismissal of the poor (his ministry pulses with justice and compassion), but an acknowledgment of a unique, unfolding moment. Mary's extravagant love meets the urgency of salvation's hour.

Meanwhile, crowds gather, not just to see Jesus but also Lazarus (proof living and breathing that death's reign is fragile), the chief priests, maddened by the loss of control, plot to kill Lazarus too. Resurrection always threatens the powers committed to death.

For our spiritual lives, this passage stands as both an invitation and an indictment. Mary's act is pure, undiluted worship. She gives what is costly, holding nothing back, unconcerned with how it looks or what others whisper. Her love is uncalculating, fragrant, a poured-out yes. In her, we see the heart of true discipleship: adoration that spills over into scandalous generosity.

It also confronts our temptation to reduce devotion to utilitarianism. Judas speaks in the language of charity, but without love, it rings hollow. Jesus wants us to serve people experiencing poverty, yes, but out of hearts captivated by him. Otherwise, even good deeds can become a means of self-gain.

And it reminds us that following Jesus will draw crowds and critics alike. The scent of resurrection disrupts settled orders. Systems built on fear and exploitation feel the tremor when Christ sits at the table, when dead men walk, when women pour out all they have for love.

As disciples, we are called to live like Mary: unclenching our grip on what's precious, unafraid to let the house fill with the aroma of our worship, trusting that nothing poured out at Jesus's feet is ever wasted.

Guiding Truth: True discipleship pours out costly love at Jesus's feet, unconcerned with appearances, trusting that nothing given to him is ever lost.

Reflection: What treasure am I still clutching, afraid to break open for Christ? How might my love for Jesus become a fragrance that fills the lives of others?

Prayer: Jesus, worth more than all my treasures, teach me to pour out my life at your feet. Let my devotion be bold and fragrant, unconcerned with whispers of waste. Make my love a sweet offering that tells your story to the world. Amen.

Day 29: The Glory of a Dying Seed

Reading: John 12:12–36

The crowd swells with longing. Palm branches wave. Shouts of "Hosanna! Blessed is the one who comes in the name of the Lord!" pierce the air. It looks like a coronation, but Jesus rides in not on a war horse but a donkey's colt. He's the King, yes, but of an upside-down kingdom.

This isn't triumph as the world expects. There are no banners of conquest, no swords, no armor. Just dust, humility, and the quiet resolve of a Messiah who will be lifted up, not on a throne, but on a cross.

The disciples don't understand it at the moment. They'll remember later: after the tomb, after the Spirit, after their dreams of greatness are buried and raised into something truer.

Some Greeks want to see Jesus. The boundaries are beginning to break. Glory is expanding beyond one people, one nation. The seed is falling to the ground.

And Jesus knows. "The hour has come for the Son of Man to be glorified." But the glory he speaks of is wrapped in paradox: "Unless a grain of wheat falls to the earth and dies, it remains alone; but if it dies, it bears much fruit."

This is the shape of divine love: surrender that multiplies, death that gives birth to life. Jesus doesn't sidestep the weight of it. His soul is troubled. He could ask to be spared. But instead, he prays, "Father, glorify your name."

A voice from heaven answers, thundering affirmation. The crowd is bewildered. Some hear thunder, others imagine angels. Revelation is always filtered through the ears of the listener.

Jesus then says something staggering: "Now is the judgment of this world; now the ruler of this world will be cast out. And I, when I'm lifted up from the earth, will draw all people to myself."

Not all will respond, but all will be summoned. All will be seen. All will be loved by a God who bleeds.

This moment matters for our spiritual lives. We want glory without grief, light without dying, calling without cost. But Jesus invites us to follow him as seeds: falling, surrendering, and trusting that what dies within us can yield something beautiful for the world.

It challenges how we live. Are we chasing power or embodying presence? Are we clinging to safety, or letting love lead us into holy risk?

The hour has come. Not just for Jesus, but for us. To lay down the illusion of control, to walk into mystery, to follow the One who turns death into fruitfulness.

Guiding Truth: Real glory doesn't cling to life but surrenders it, trusting that love buried in the ground will rise again.

Reflection: Where am I resisting the call to die to self, to control, to comfort? What might God grow from the seed I'm being asked to plant?

Prayer: Jesus, you rode into the noise and the misunderstanding, knowing the cross awaited. Help me follow you: not with palm branches alone, but with a life laid down in sacrifice. Make me like the seed, surrendered, hidden, and alive with your promise. Amen.

Day 30: Light That Won't Be Silenced

Reading: John 12:37–50

The signs had been given. The blind received sight. The dead were raised. Bread was multiplied. Still, many refused to believe. Not because the evidence was lacking, but because belief comes at a cost.

John doesn't flinch. He names the truth with sorrow: some hearts are hardened. Some eyes prefer darkness. Some systems are so invested in power and reputation that they can't welcome a suffering Messiah who disarms both.

Quoting Isaiah, John reminds us that this isn't new. Prophets were always resisted. Light has always met resistance. The arm of the Lord is revealed but not always embraced.

And yet, some did believe, even among the leaders. But fear bound their tongues. "They loved human glory more than the glory that comes from God." That sentence should make us tremble because it names a temptation that lives in all of us: to stay silent when we should speak, to prioritize our platform over living the truth, and to seek applause instead of authenticity.

Jesus cries out, no longer speaking in parables or quiet metaphors, but with clarity and urgency. "Whoever believes in me doesn't believe in me only, but in the One who sent me." His life is the reflection of God's heart. To see Jesus is to know the One who sent him.

Then comes the thunderclap: "I have come into the world as light, so that no one who believes in me should stay in darkness." There's no condemnation in that sentence, only an invitation. Light has come. Not to shame, but to awaken. Not to wound, but to heal.

Jesus doesn't judge according to ego or empire. His judgment is love exposed: truth held up against illusion. The word he speaks is the word that will stand, not as a weapon, but as a mirror.

This passage prompts us to consider where we still hide in shadows, where we resist the cost of courageous belief, and where we bow to cultural approval, avoiding the risk of bearing witness.

It also reminds us that Jesus doesn't wield light as a sword, but as a gift. He comes not to destroy, but to draw. His mission isn't rooted in vengeance but in mercy that burns like fire: cleansing, clarifying, consuming what can't remain.

For all our complexity, Jesus remains astonishingly clear: to follow him is to walk in light. And that light may expose us, but it will also heal us.

Guiding Truth: The light of Christ reveals what's true, not to shame us, but to free us and invite us to walk courageously in the open.

Reflection: Where am I hiding behind reputation, silence, or fear? What might it look like to walk fully in the light of Christ today?

Prayer: Jesus, you are the light that can't be quenched. Shine into my fears, my compromises, and my shadows. Give me the courage to speak what is true, to love what is right, and to follow you wherever your light leads. Amen.

Day 31: The Towel, the Basin, and the Betrayer

Reading: John 13:1–20

The hour has come.

Not the hour of coronation, but the hour of descent. Of vulnerability. Of surrender. Jesus knows that his time has arrived. The cross looms. Yet in this moment, before betrayal and arrest, he chooses a towel over a throne, a basin over applause.

He gets up from the table, takes off his outer garment, and kneels to wash the dust from his disciples' feet. It's not just an act of kindness. It's a revolution in cloth and water. The teacher becomes the servant. The Holy bends low.

Feet are strange things: dusty, cracked, unclean. And yet Jesus touches them all. Even Judas. Even Peter. Even the ones who will scatter in fear. He washes what the world avoids. He cleanses what pride refuses to touch.

Peter objects. He wants Jesus to remain exalted, not kneeling. But Jesus gently insists: "Unless I wash you, you have no share with me." This is more than hygiene. It's participation. Union. Surrender.

Jesus is forming a community not of power, but of downward love, and a people who don't seek status but stoop to serve. He isn't just teaching service; he's embodying divine humility. This is what glory looks like when stripped of illusion.

Afterward, he says, "Do you understand what I've done?" He doesn't ask if they admired him, but if they'll follow. "I've set an example." Not of mere niceness, but of radical reorientation. The kind that dismantles hierarchy and honors the lowly.

And then this startling line: "Blessed are you if you do them." Not know them. Do them. Theology must become foot washing. Revelation must become a rag in hand. Orthodoxy must kneel.

This passage isn't a soft prelude to the Passion. It's the center of the gospel. If we skip the towel, we misunderstand the cross. If we avoid the basin, we distort resurrection.

Jesus washes even the one who will betray him. Grace, poured like water, reaches into treachery. He loves to the end. And still invites: "Follow me."

Guiding Truth: To walk with Jesus is to kneel with him; to serve in humility, love without condition, and lead by stooping low.

Reflection: What parts of me resist the humility of foot washing love? Whom am I being called to serve, not in theory, but in flesh-and-blood humility?

Prayer: Jesus, Servant and Savior, teach me to love as you do. Strip me of pride. Bend my life toward mercy. May I not only believe in you but follow you to the towel, to the basin, and to the cross. Amen.

Day 32: The Betrayal Foretold, the Denial Exposed

Reading: John 13:21–38

The room is thick with tension. Jesus has just washed their feet (every one of them), including the one preparing to betray him. Now, grief stirs within him. "One of you will betray me." A crack runs through the table. The disciples shift. Eyes dart. Hearts pound. Trust trembles.

John, leaning against Jesus, becomes the conduit for the question none dare voice aloud: "Lord, who is it?" Jesus answers with a sign: a piece of bread dipped and handed to Judas. A final gesture of intimacy. And yet, "Satan entered into him." Betrayal begins not with hatred but with a slow resistance to love.

Jesus turns to Judas: "What you're about to do, do quickly." And Judas leaves. "It was night." Not just chronologically. Spiritually. Darkness falls where love is refused.

But Jesus doesn't dwell in that night. He immediately speaks of glory. Not despite betrayal, but through it. "Now the Son of Man is glorified." The cross looms larger now, and Jesus walks toward it, not with dread, but with love ablaze.

Then, another shock: "Where I'm going, you can't follow now." Peter, loyal and impulsive, declares: "I'll lay down my life for you." And Jesus, with sorrow, tells him the truth: "Before the rooster crows, you'll disown me three times."

This chapter is a mirror. It reflects our Judas-moments: when we turn away from costly love. It also reflects our Peter-moments: when our devotion outpaces our courage. Jesus names them both, not to shame, but to invite honesty. To walk with Jesus isn't about never failing; it's about being known in our weakness and still being loved.

This passage pulls no punches. It reminds us that betrayal can come from within, that self-confidence is fragile, and that following Jesus requires more than emotion; it demands a cross-shaped trust.

And yet, in the face of all this (betrayal, denial, darkness) Jesus stays. He continues to love. He speaks of glory. He looks into fragile hearts and offers grace.

Here, we're reminded that discipleship isn't about spiritual bravado, but rather about daily surrender. It's not about never stumbling but always returning.

Guiding Truth: Jesus loves us even through betrayal and denial and invites us into grace that meets us in the night.

Reflection: Where am I tempted to profess bold faith but withhold costly trust? In what ways is Jesus asking me to be honest about my fragility and receive grace?

Prayer: Jesus, you see the Judas in me and the Peter too. Still, you love. Still, you invite. Teach me to stay near, to confess honestly, and to follow with humility and hope, even when I've stumbled. Amen.

Day 33: The Way, the Truth, and the Homecoming

Reading: John 14:1–14

"Don't let your hearts be troubled." These words ring out like a deep bell in a storm. Jesus speaks to them not in ease but on the eve of betrayal, denial, and death. In the shadow of the cross, he offers comfort: not by minimizing pain but by reminding us of presence. "You believe in God; believe also in me."

He speaks of a house with many rooms, a home expansive enough to hold all our grief, our hope, our becoming. A place prepared, not by divine magic, but by divine self-giving. "I go to prepare a place for you." The preparation is the cross. The path is painful. But the destination is communion.

Thomas voices what many feel: "We don't know where you're going. How can we know the way?" It's the honest cry of a bewildered heart. And Jesus responds not with a map, but with himself: "I'm the way, and the truth, and the life." The journey isn't toward a set of doctrines, but into a relationship. The way isn't abstract; it's embodied. The truth isn't cold; it's compassionate. Life isn't distant; it's deeply near.

Then comes Philip: "Show us the Father." A request that holds generations of longing. And Jesus says, "If you've seen me, you've seen the Father." What is God like? Look at Jesus: serving, forgiving, weeping, breaking bread, embracing outcasts, standing with the wounded. The divine mystery isn't locked in a scroll or shielded by smoke. It's made flesh and bone, voice and touch, in Christ.

These verses draw us into a radical claim: God isn't aloof. God is revealed in Jesus: in vulnerability, justice, humility, and glory.

But Jesus doesn't stop there. He invites us into participation: "The one who believes in me will do the works that I do: even greater." Not because we're greater, but because the Spirit will dwell in us. This isn't a call to power but to faithfulness. It's a summons to carry Christ's healing, hope, and justice into a hurting world.

This passage comforts, challenges, and commissions. It says to the troubled heart: You're not alone. It calls the fearful disciple to courage: "I'm the way." And it sends us out with purpose: "You'll do my works."

Guiding Truth: Jesus isn't just a guide, but the path, the home, and the heart of God, inviting us to follow, believe, and live as His embodied presence in the world.

Reflection: Where in my life am I looking for the way when Jesus is already walking beside me? How is God calling me to participate in Christ's works of love, justice, and healing?

Prayer: Jesus, my Way and my Truth, draw my troubled heart into your peace. Let me trust your presence more than my confusion. Teach me to live as your hands and voice, bearing your light in places of fear and need. Amen.

Day 34: The Spirit Who Comes to Stay

Reading: John 14:15–31

"If you love me, you'll keep my commandments." These words, often misread as transactional, are profoundly relational. Jesus isn't setting conditions; he's describing a reality. Love and obedience aren't separate tracks; they're intertwined. Love leads to listening and listening leads to a life formed by the Way.

But Jesus knows love alone won't sustain the disciples in what's ahead. So, he promises another Advocate. One who won't leave. One who won't just walk beside us, but dwell within us. This isn't some abstract force or fleeting inspiration; it's the Spirit of truth, presence, and divine intimacy. The Spirit isn't given to the world's systems of power and pretense but to those who love, seek, and follow.

"I won't leave you as orphans." In a world fractured by abandonment and loneliness, this is gospel. Christ's departure isn't an ending; it's the beginning of a deeper presence. The Spirit doesn't merely remind us of Jesus's teachings; the Spirit reveals Jesus to us, again and again, in real time, in the grit and glory of daily life.

The peace Jesus gives isn't like the peace offered by empires and economies. It isn't the absence of trouble; it's the presence of God in the midst of it. "Don't let your hearts be troubled, and don't let them be afraid." This isn't a demand to suppress fear but an invitation to live anchored in something more profound than fear.

Obedience here isn't about rule-keeping but union. The one who keeps Christ's word is drawn into a communion so profound that the divine will make a home within them. This isn't a metaphor. It's incarnation: God dwelling not just in Christ, but in every follower who abides in love and truth.

Jesus speaks all this, knowing what's ahead. The cross looms. Betrayal is underway. And still, he speaks of peace, presence, love, and Spirit. This isn't the language of a desperate teacher. This is the voice of One who reigns through surrender, who wins through love, who builds a kingdom not of control but of communion.

This passage isn't just theology. It's a blueprint for discipleship in a time of absence and confusion. Love. Listen. Receive the Spirit. Live with peace. Keep going.

Guiding Truth: The Spirit isn't a distant mystery but God-with-us: dwelling in those who love, guiding us in truth, and forming Christ within.

Reflection: Where am I tempted to seek peace the world gives instead of the peace Jesus offers? How is the Spirit inviting me into deeper obedience born of love, not fear?

Prayer: Holy Spirit, come and dwell, not as a guest, but as life itself. Let your peace anchor me, your truth guide me, and your presence shape me. Teach me to love with my whole life. Let me carry your flame into a world starved for light. Amen.

Day 35: Abide and Bear Fruit

Reading: John 15:1–17

"I'm the true vine," Jesus says, and with that one phrase, he reorders everything. He isn't just a teacher of wisdom or a miracle-worker with crowds. He's the source. The life. The root. And we (we aren't independent stalks, not wild branches), we're meant to remain in him.

This isn't a call to spiritual effort but to spiritual union. "Abide in me," Jesus urges. Remain. Stay. Dwell. It's the posture of trust, the rhythm of surrender. To abide is to resist the temptation of hurried faith, of transactional religion, of roots in shallow soil. It's to stay with Christ in the long, slow work of love.

The Father, Jesus says, is the gardener. There's pruning involved. Cutting back. Stripping down. Even the fruitful branches are trimmed so they might bear more. Pain isn't always punishment. Sometimes it's preparation. Sometimes, pruning is how life multiplies.

And here's the paradox: we long for lives that matter, but the way to fruitfulness isn't striving, it's abiding. It's not about doing more. It's about remaining rooted. Without the vine, we can do nothing. But in him, our lives pulse with grace and fruit that endures.

And what is this fruit? Love. The kind that lays itself down. The type that washes feet and welcomes outcasts. The kind that gives itself away in humble service of the forgotten, least, marginalized, exploited, oppressed, and last. The type that bears another's burden and speaks truth with tenderness. This isn't sentimental affection; it's covenantal love, sacrificial love, world-reversing love. "Love one another as I have loved you." This is the heart of the gospel.

Jesus says, "I no longer call you servants . . . but friends." Not because the work is done but because the relationship has deepened. We aren't tools in a mission; we're beloved companions in a divine story.

This kind of friendship costs something. "Greater love has no one than this: to lay down one's life for one's friends." This isn't theoretical. Jesus is walking toward the cross. He's about to embody everything he's just spoken. And he invites us into that same pattern of love: marked by abiding, shaped by pruning, and overflowing in fruit.

This passage isn't about achieving. It's about remaining. And when we remain, fruit comes not always quickly, not always visibly, but deeply and truly. It's not about success. It's about communion. The goal isn't performance but love.

Guiding Truth: True discipleship flows from abiding in Christ, where love takes root, fruit is born, and joy becomes complete.

Reflection: Where am I striving instead of abiding? How is God inviting me to be pruned so that love might flourish more fully in me?

Prayer: Jesus, Vine of life, teach me to remain. Cut away what doesn't bear fruit. Root me deeply in your love. Let every part of my life grow from your presence, and bear fruit that blesses the world. Amen.

Day 36: Hated but Held

Reading: John 15:18–27

"If the world hates you, keep in mind that it hated me first." These aren't the words of a leader promising comfort or popularity. They're the sober truth of a kingdom that stands in contrast to every system built on self-interest, domination, and pride.

Jesus is clear: alignment with him means misalignment with the powers that oppose love, truth, and mercy. Following him will provoke resistance: not because we're seeking conflict, but because light exposes what darkness prefers to keep hidden.

The world's hostility toward Jesus wasn't abstract: it came through ridicule, exclusion, betrayal, and violence. He tells his disciples to expect the same. Yet he also promises that they'll never face this alone. "When the Advocate comes," he says, "the Spirit of truth who goes out from the Father, he'll testify about me."

The Spirit doesn't just comfort; the Spirit strengthens, emboldens, and gives words when our courage falters. Our witness isn't self-generated: it's Spirit-born. We testify to Christ because the Spirit testifies within us.

This passage also warns against selective discipleship. We can't fully appreciate the beauty of Jesus's teaching while rejecting the cost of following it. Love in the pattern of Christ will inevitably draw resistance. The question isn't whether we'll be liked, but whether we'll be faithful.

Here's the paradox: persecution doesn't mean the absence of God's blessing: it can mean the presence of God's kingdom breaking into the world. Hatred from the powers isn't proof of failure; it's often confirmation that we belong to another way entirely.

To follow Jesus is to stand in the tension: misunderstood by many, embraced by few, yet held in the unbreakable grip of God's Spirit. We're called to bear witness with humility, truth, and courage, knowing that our words and lives may be the only gospel some will see.

Guiding Truth: Faithfulness to Christ may bring opposition, but the Spirit's presence empowers us to bear witness with courage and love.

Reflection: Where am I tempted to compromise truth for acceptance? How can I lean on the Spirit's strength when facing resistance to my faith?

Prayer: Spirit of truth, anchor me when the winds of opposition rise. Give me courage to speak, patience to endure, and love that never retaliates. Let my witness honor Jesus, even in the face of rejection. Amen.

Day 37: Sorrow, Spirit, and the Truth That Sets Free

Reading: John 16:1–15

Jesus speaks to his disciples with unflinching honesty and tender love. He doesn't pretend the road ahead will be smooth. He warns them they'll be excluded from the synagogue, cut off from the center of their religious community, and even face death from people convinced they're serving God. The shock isn't just that persecution will come it's that people will do it in the name of righteousness. By telling them this before it happens, Jesus offers a gift: the ability to remember, amid trial, that none of it has caught him off guard.

Then comes one of the most paradoxical statements in the Gospels: "It's for your good that I'm going away." The disciples can't imagine how his absence could be an advantage. Yet Jesus knows that his physical departure will make way for the arrival of the Advocate (the Spirit of truth) who'll be present not just beside them, but within them.

The Spirit's coming isn't merely for comfort; it's for transformation and confrontation. The Spirit will convict the world, pulling back the curtain on sin, showing that righteousness is found in Jesus alone, and announcing the ultimate defeat of the powers that oppose God. Conviction here isn't condemnation; it's a loving exposure of what is false, so that truth and life can take root.

The Spirit's work doesn't stop at conviction. Jesus promises that the Spirit will guide his followers into all truth: not by revealing every future detail in one overwhelming download, but by walking with them, step by step, revealing what they need in the moment they need it. Truth, in this vision, isn't something we master; it's Someone we follow.

And the Spirit never speaks independently, as a separate voice. Every word, prompting, or whisper of the Spirit is rooted in Jesus himself. The Spirit takes what belongs to Jesus (his words, works, and heart) and makes it known to us in living, personal ways.

This passage calls us to openness and surrender. Hearts already crowded with self-sufficiency, pride, or fear will struggle to receive the Spirit's leading. But those who yield (those willing to be searched, corrected, and redirected) find themselves drawn deeper into the life of Christ.

Jesus's words remind us that sorrow can have purpose, and loss can lead to presence. Even in seasons of uncertainty or grief, the Spirit comes to continue the work of Jesus in us and through us, shaping us into people who carry truth not as a weapon, but as a healing presence in the world.

Guiding Truth: The Spirit of truth comes to comfort, convict, and guide, carrying the life of Jesus into our hearts and through our lives.

Reflection: Where am I resisting the Spirit's guidance because it disrupts my comfort? How might I make space for the Spirit to lead me more fully into the truth of Jesus?

Prayer: Spirit of truth, unsettle my complacency and lead me into the life of Christ. Give me ears to hear your voice and courage to follow where you lead. Let my life be a vessel of your conviction, comfort, and guidance. Amen.

Day 38: Sorrow That Turns to Joy

Reading: John 16:16–33

Jesus speaks in language that confuses the disciples: "In a little while you will see me no more, and then after a little while you will see me." They whisper among themselves, trying to make sense of it. The words feel like a riddle, but they are a doorway into the mystery of the cross and resurrection. Jesus is preparing them for the anguish of his death and for the joy that will burst forth when he is alive again.

He uses the image of a woman in labor. Pain fills the moment, but the moment isn't the end. It's a passage. Labor hurts because something new is being born. For the disciples, grief will feel crushing. But it won't have the last word. Resurrection will turn sorrow into joy no one can steal.

This isn't joy that ignores pain. It's joy that comes through pain. Jesus doesn't promise escape from the brokenness of the world; he promises a kind of joy that's deeper than the world's power to take it away.

Then Jesus speaks of prayer in his name. Until now, the disciples have asked him directly. Soon, they'll pray to the Father in his name and be heard not as outsiders hoping for favor, but as beloved ones welcomed into the inner life of God. "The Father himself loves you," he tells them. Not loves you if, not loves you when: loves you now, because you have trusted me.

Yet he doesn't soften the reality ahead. "In this world, you'll have trouble." He names it plainly. Faith isn't insulation from hardship; it's a lifeline in it. Trouble will come, but despair doesn't have to. Why? "Take heart! I've overcome the world."

Overcoming here isn't a clenched-fist victory of domination. It's the victory of self-giving love, of a cross that dismantles the powers of sin and death. It's the triumph of a kingdom that doesn't rise by the sword but by sacrifice.

This passage is a call to endurance and trust. It invites us to believe that our deepest sorrows can be transformed into joy: not by pretending they don't hurt, but by allowing them to be met by the resurrection life of Jesus. It calls us to prayer that is rooted in intimacy, not transaction. And it anchors us in the unshakable truth that Jesus has already overcome, even when our circumstances seem to say otherwise.

The world's trouble is real. But the victory of Jesus is more real still.

Guiding Truth: Jesus turns our deepest sorrows into unshakable joy and calls us to live in the peace of his victory.

Reflection: Where do I need to let sorrow become a passage rather than a prison? How can I pray with greater trust in the Creator's love and Jesus's victory?

Prayer: Risen Lord, hold my heart in your peace when the world shakes. Turn my grief into joy. Teach me to pray from the place of being loved. Keep my eyes fixed on your victory, not my fear. Amen.

Day 39: Glory in the Hour of the Cross

Reading: John 17:1–5

Jesus lifts his eyes toward heaven and begins to pray not in private, but within earshot of his disciples. These words open what's often called the High Priestly Prayer, the longest recorded prayer of Jesus in the Gospels. And in these opening lines, we hear the heartbeat of his mission.

"The hour has come." All through John's Gospel, Jesus has spoken of "the hour" as something still in the future: the appointed time when his work would reach its climax. Now, the waiting is over. This isn't the hour of political triumph, not the hour of worldly acclaim, but the hour of the cross. In Jesus's vision, glory and crucifixion aren't opposites; they're bound together. The cross isn't the end of his glory but the revelation of it.

He prays, "Glorify your Son, that your Son may glorify you." Glory here isn't ego or self-promotion. It's the radiant display of God's self-giving love. In being "lifted up" on the cross, Jesus will make visible the nature of God: a love willing to bear the cost of redemption.

Jesus grounds his prayer in the authority given to him "over all people," authority not to dominate but to give eternal life. And eternal life, as Jesus defines it, isn't simply endless existence; it's relational knowing: "that they know you, the only true God, and Jesus Christ whom you have sent." Eternal life isn't a distant reward; it begins now in the deep, ongoing intimacy between Creator and creation, made possible through Christ.

He declares that he has finished the work given to him. This isn't the resignation of someone giving up; it's the satisfaction of someone who has fully lived into their calling. Every sign, every teaching, every healing, every act of mercy has been leading here.

Finally, Jesus asks to return to the glory he had with the Father before the world began. This isn't a request to escape the world, but to complete the circle: to move through the cross into the fullness of shared glory, the divine communion that has no beginning or end.

For us, these words draw our eyes to the paradox at the center of the Gospel: that the greatest revelation of God's glory is found not in power as the world defines it, but in self-emptying love. This challenges our understanding of success, status, and what it means to live a life that glorifies God.

To follow Jesus is to embrace a glory that the world may never applaud: a glory that's humble, sacrificial, and wholly rooted in the love that flows between Father and Son, and now through us.

Guiding Truth: The glory of God is revealed most fully in the self-giving love of Jesus, who invites us into eternal life through knowing him.

Reflection: How does my life define glory, and does it align with Jesus's definition? What might it look like for me to glorify God in the ordinary and costly moments of life?

Prayer: Lord of glory, teach me to see beauty in the cross and splendor in humility. Draw me into the eternal life of knowing you deeply. May my days reflect your love and reveal your heart to the world. Amen.

Day 40: Kept in the Name

Reading: John 17:6–19

Jesus continues his prayer, shifting the focus to those the Father has given him. The intimacy here is staggering. Jesus speaks of the disciples as a gift, entrusted to him, kept in the Father's name. They have received his words, believed that he came from God, and now bear the weight of his mission.

"I'm not praying for the world," Jesus says, not because the world is excluded from God's love, but because this prayer is for the ones who will carry that love into the world. He asks not for their removal from danger but for their protection in it. This is the realism of Jesus: discipleship will place them in the path of hostility, misunderstanding, and rejection. Yet he prays they'll be "kept from the evil one," guarded not by isolation but by the truth.

"Sanctify them in the truth; your word is truth." Sanctification here isn't about withdrawal into a cloistered life but about being set apart for holy purpose right amid the world's mess. Truth isn't an abstract concept; truth is embodied in Jesus himself. To be sanctified in truth is to be shaped, sustained, and sent by the life and words of Christ.

Jesus knows the tensions his followers will face. They're "not of the world" in their values and allegiance, yet they're still in the world, embedded in its cultures, economies, and systems. Their identity must be anchored in God's kingdom so they're not swept into the current of fear, greed, or violence.

As the Father sent Jesus, so Jesus sends them. The mission flows directly from the character of God: a love that enters, engages, and redeems rather than retreats. This sending is costly. It'll require courage to confront lies with truth, hope to challenge despair, and humility to serve without seeking recognition.

In this prayer, we see Jesus's confidence that the Father's keeping is stronger than any threat. His disciples aren't preserved so they can remain safe in private devotion; God preserves them so they can bear witness in public faithfulness.

For us, these words are both a comfort and a commission. Jesus doesn't abandon us in our calling. God's keeping is real, active, and unbreakable. But that keeping is never an excuse for passivity. It's the security from which we move into the world with the truth and love of Christ.

To be "kept in the name" is to live under God's character and authority, to embody divine compassion, justice, and mercy in every sphere of life. And to be sanctified in truth is to let our lives bear witness to the One who sends us still.

Guiding Truth: God's keeping empowers our sending. Sanctified in truth, God calls us to live out the mission of Christ in the world.

Reflection: What would change if I truly believed I was "kept" by God in every circumstance? How can I live as one sanctified in truth in my relationships, work, and witness?

Prayer: Faithful Keeper, root me in your truth and send me into the world with courage. Protect me from fear and make my life a testimony to your love and justice. Amen.

Day 41: The Glory That Makes Us One

Reading: John 17:20–26

Jesus's prayer widens. No longer only for the disciples in front of him, he now prays for *all* who will believe through their message, including us. Across centuries and cultures, his voice reaches forward to gather every follower into this moment.

The heartbeat of the prayer is unity: not uniformity, but a profound oneness rooted in the shared life of Father, Son, and Spirit. "That they may all be one," Jesus prays, "just as you, Father, are in me, and I in you." This isn't a call to bland agreement or institutional sameness. It's an invitation into the relational life of God: a unity forged in love, sustained by truth, and made visible in our life together.

This unity isn't for our comfort; it's for the sake of the world. "So that the world may believe that you have sent me." When believers live in reconciled, self-giving relationships, they bear credible witness to God's reconciling mission. When we divide along lines of pride, power, or preference, we obscure the gospel's beauty.

Jesus speaks of giving us the same glory the Father gave him: not glory as domination or celebrity, but the glory of sacrificial love, radiant humility, and steadfast obedience. This glory binds us to him and each other, empowering us to live as a foretaste of God's new creation.

He desires that we would be with him, to see his glory fully revealed. This is the longing at the center of the universe: to dwell with God in unhindered fellowship, where love is the atmosphere and joy is complete. Eternal life isn't merely unending existence; it's the shared life of God flowing without barrier between Creator and creation.

Jesus closes with a final affirmation: "I 've made your name known to them, and will continue to make it known, so that the love you have for me may be in them, and I in them." This is the essence of discipleship: not merely knowing facts about God but being indwelt by the very love of God.

For us, this prayer is both promise and calling. We're held in the unity of the Triune God, drawn into a love that transcends every wall we build. Our task is to live into that unity (actively, intentionally, and humbly) so the world sees in us a reflection of Jesus's reconciling heart.

We can't manufacture this unity. It's a gift we receive, a reality we embody, and a witness we protect. In a fractured world, one of the most radical acts of discipleship is to remain united in love while holding fast to truth. This is the unity that Jesus prayed into being, and it's still his longing for us today.

Guiding Truth: The unity Jesus prayed for is rooted in God's love, empowered by God's glory, and given for the sake of the world's faith.

Reflection: Where am I resisting the unity Christ has already given? What would it look like to embody God's love in a way that draws others toward belief?

Prayer: Lord of glory, draw me deeper into your love until it flows freely to others. Make my life a witness to your reconciling heart. Keep me rooted in the unity you prayed for, that the world may believe. Amen.

Day 42: The Garden, the Trial, and the Rooster's Cry

Reading: John 18:1–27

Night settles over the olive grove. A place of prayer becomes a place of arrest. Lanterns flicker through the trees, and the quiet is shattered by the sound of footsteps and steel. At the front is Judas, leading soldiers and officials. He comes not with truth but with treachery, trading intimacy for advantage.

Jesus steps forward: no cowering, no retreat. "Who are you looking for?" he asks. "Jesus of Nazareth," they answer. "I am," Jesus replies, echoing the divine name that once thundered from the burning bush. The sheer weight of the words knocks them backward. Power stands unarmed, yet nothing can touch him until he surrenders.

Peter, still clinging to the way of the sword, strikes a servant. But Jesus rebukes him and heals the wound. Here's a kingdom that won't be defended by violence. The cup must be drunk; the way of the cross can't be avoided.

Bound, Jesus is taken to the high priest. Interrogations begin. False accusations swirl. He speaks the truth plainly, but they don't hear. This is the nature of hardened power: it can't bear the light.

Meanwhile, Peter waits outside. Three times, he's asked if he knows Jesus. Three times, he denies it. The crowing of a rooster punctuates the final denial. And Luke tells us that in that moment, Jesus turned and looked at him. Imagine that gaze: piercing, knowing, merciful. Not the stare of condemnation, but the eyes of one who had already prayed for Peter's restoration.

This passage is a mirror. Judas's betrayal, Peter's denial, the leaders' rejection: they're not just historical failures. They expose our hearts. We, too, are tempted to betray in subtle ways: when allegiance to Jesus conflicts with our comfort, when speaking the truth might cost us influence, and when we prioritize self-protection over costly love.

But the story isn't simply about failure; it's about the steadfastness of Christ. He doesn't flinch from the cross. He doesn't abandon his friends, even as they abandon him. His mercy reaches into the very moments when we are least faithful, holding us until we return.

For disciples today, this passage calls us to examine the ways we resist the path of the cross. It invites us to lay down the swords of defensiveness, control, and fear, and to follow Jesus into the way of truth and self-giving love. And when we fail (as we will), it calls us to return, trusting the gaze of mercy more than the shame of our denial.

Guiding Truth: Even in our betrayal and denial, Jesus remains faithful, calling us to abandon violence, speak truth, and trust his mercy.

Reflection: Where am I grasping for control instead of surrendering to God's way? How might I respond differently when fear tempts me to deny Christ?

Prayer: Jesus, you meet my failures with mercy. Break my grip on power and fear. Teach me to follow your way of truth and peace. And when I falter, I turn my eyes toward yours until I find my way home. Amen.

Day 43: A Kingdom Not of This World

Reading: John 18:28–40

The religious elite deliver Jesus to the headquarters of the empire. They won't enter, lest they be defiled before the Passover. So, they stand outside, clean on the surface, while handing over the Innocent One to the machinery of death.

Hypocrisy is never subtle. It can recite sacred texts while sharpening spears. It can keep ritual laws while plotting executions. And yet, Jesus remains silent before their doublemindedness, allowing the fullness of their contradictions to speak for themselves.

Pilate emerges confused, pragmatic, manipulative, tired, and jaded. "Are you the King of the Jews?" he asks, not out of faith but politics. He wants to size Jesus up, to see if he's a threat to Roman order or just another fringe mystic.

Jesus doesn't give him a straight answer. He never plays the game of empire. Instead, he speaks of a kingdom not from this world: a kingdom that doesn't come with legions or propaganda, with coercion or crowns. A kingdom rooted in truth.

Pilate scoffs, "What's truth?" The line is weary, cynical, and terrifyingly modern. Pilate names what many in our culture live: not the absence of truth, but the suspicion that truth is unknowable or irrelevant. In a world addicted to spin, to image, to algorithmic manipulation, the idea of truth sounds like fiction.

But Jesus doesn't flinch. He doesn't explain truth as a concept; he embodies it. The truth stands bloodied and bound before the power structures of the world, quietly proclaiming love is stronger than fear, sacrifice is stronger than violence, and truth will outlast every lie.

Pilate, strangely moved, finds no guilt in Jesus. He tries to offer an out. "Do you want me to release the King of the Jews?" But the people, stirred by their leaders, cry out for Barabbas instead. We shouldn't be surprised; crowds are often fickle and easily swayed by collective fervor and sentiment.

Barabbas is a violent rebel and a murderer. Jesus is the Prince of Peace, the giver of life. The crowd chooses Barabbas. They always do. Because empires understand power, not mercy. Empires prefer force over grace, certainty over mystery, and violence over mercy.

And still, Jesus doesn't resist. He doesn't beg. He doesn't argue. The silence of Christ is the loudest word in the room.

This passage isn't just history; it's a diagnosis. We live in a world that chooses Barabbas every day, that fears the gentle strength of Jesus, that dresses injustice in religious robes and calls it righteousness, and that echoes Pilate's shrug: "What's truth?"

But for those with ears to hear, Jesus is still speaking. His kingdom isn't built with violence or fear, but with truth, love, and the cross. It isn't from this world, but it's very much for it.

Guiding Truth: Christ's kingdom doesn't mimic the world's power: it embodies truth, mercy, and sacrificial love.

Reflection: Where am I tempted to choose Barabbas: opting for control over surrender? How might I live into the truth of Christ's kingdom in a culture that scoffs at truth?

Prayer: Jesus, you're the truth the world can't grasp. Teach me to resist the pull of violent power and empty religion. Anchor me in your kingdom: not of this world, but alive within it. Amen.

Day 44: The Crown, the Cross, and the Final Gift

Reading: John 19:1–27

The scene is thick with cruelty and irony. A crown woven from thorns is pressed into Jesus's flesh, a robe thrown over torn shoulders, and mockery poured out like vinegar on open wounds. They mock and torment the Lord of the heavens and the earth, and they don't know it. The One who flung galaxies into being is paraded before the crowd, bruised and bleeding, as if powerless. Yet every lash and every taunt moves history toward its deepest truth.

Pilate presents him: "Behold the man." It's more than politics; it's prophecy. Here stands humanity as God intended and humanity as humanity has made it: the image of divine love, bearing the violence of our rebellion. The crowd cries for execution. Pilate washes his hands in cowardice. The empire flexes: religion conspires. Love remains.

Jesus carries the cross to the place of the skull. There, nails fasten flesh to wood, and the world sees love lifted high. Over his head, a sign reads, "King of the Jews." It's meant to shame; it declares the truth. His throne is suffering; his coronation is death. This is the God of all creation and the Lord of all humanity acting in ways that confound our understanding of power, authority, and might. Instead of using that glory as we'd expect, Jesus reveals God as vulnerable, loving, merciful, pained, and suffering.

In agony, he sees his mother. With one of his last breaths, he entrusts her to the beloved disciple. Even here, love is practical, intimate, and embodied. In the shadow of cosmic salvation, he makes sure the vulnerable are cared for. This is the kingdom: not only the redemption of the world but the protection of the one standing before you.

At the cross, God's justice and mercy meet. This isn't a transaction; it's the revelation of a kingdom unlike any other. Power is redefined. Greatness is recast. Glory is reframed through the lens of sacrifice. God reveals Godself in astonishing, surprising, history-remaking ways.

We are left with a choice: Will we stand in the crowd and join the chants, hide in the distance to save ourselves, or draw near to the cross and receive both its wound and its wonder?

Guiding Truth: The cross reveals a kingdom where love suffers for the beloved and calls us to stand near those who suffer.

Reflection: Where am I tempted to seek power without the cross, glory without sacrifice? Who has God placed near me to care for, even in my season of struggle?

Prayer: Crucified King, let me not look away. Keep me near your cross, where pride dies and love lives. Teach me to carry the burdens of others with tenderness, and to entrust all things into your keeping. May I learn to follow the suffering, vulnerable, self-sacrificial, loving God. Amen.

Day 45: It Is Finished

Reading: John 19:28–42

The hours of agony stretch long. Breath comes ragged, each word costly. And yet, even in this moment of unraveling, Jesus is attentive. "I thirst," he says. It's a cry of human need, but also a fulfillment of Scripture. He takes sour wine from a sponge, his parched lips brushing against the bitter taste of this world's cruelty. Even thirst becomes part of the redeeming work.

Then, with a loud voice that cuts through despair, he declares: "It's finished." These aren't words of defeat. They're a victory cry. The work entrusted to him (the bearing of sin, the unveiling of love, the reconciliation of the world) is complete. The curtain of separation is gone forever. The kingdom is inaugurated not with fanfare but with blood and water flowing from his side. Out of his pierced body comes cleansing, renewal, and birth for a new humanity.

Those standing near testify to what they see: blood and water mingled, a fountain of life from the brokenness of death. John insists this testimony is true, that we might believe. It matters that God's salvation isn't abstract. It's tangible, embodied, and marked by wounds and witness.

Joseph of Arimathea, once fearful, steps forward. Nicodemus, who once came in secret, brings spices in abundance. Courage rises in unexpected places. These men, formerly cautious and hidden, now claim the crucified body, honoring him with dignity when the world has stripped him bare. They risk association with the condemned. They bury God's Son in a garden tomb, surrounded by the scent of myrrh and aloes.

The irony is thick: the Lord of life wrapped in grave clothes, the one who called Lazarus forth, now bound in silence. The King of glory lies in a borrowed tomb, waiting for dawn. But in that waiting, seeds are sown. Faith deepens. Courage awakens. Love refuses to let death have the final word.

This passage speaks into our lives with quiet but urgent force. To follow Jesus is to believe that the cross is enough: that God has finished the work of salvation. It's to trust that love poured out won't return empty. And it's to live like Joseph and Nicodemus, stepping out of fear into bold, tender action, even when hope seems buried.

At the tomb, we learn what discipleship requires: courage to stand with the shamed, devotion to honor what the world discards, faith to believe that silence isn't the end. The cross calls us to a life shaped by love's completion, a life that leans forward into resurrection even when the stone is still in place.

Guiding Truth: The finished work of Christ calls us to courageous faith that tends to love even when hope appears buried.

Reflection: Where in my life do I need to trust that "it's finished" is already true? What bold, tender act of discipleship is God calling me to when the world chooses fear?

Prayer: Jesus, whose love is complete, let me trust your finished work. Please give me the courage of Joseph, the devotion of Nicodemus, and the faith to honor your presence in places that seem hopeless. Teach me to wait in love for the dawn of resurrection. Amen.

Day 46: The First Word of Resurrection

Reading: John 20:1–18

Before the sun rises, Mary Magdalene walks to the tomb. The air is still heavy with grief. She comes not expecting joy but to weep, to linger near the place where love was buried. Yet when she arrives, the stone is rolled away. The silence of death has been disturbed. Imagine her horror and surprise, believing that something has happened to her Lord.

She runs to tell Peter and the beloved disciple, who sprint to the tomb. They stoop low, peering into the hollow space. Linen lies folded. Burial cloths are set aside. Something has happened here, something orderly and deliberate, not the chaos of grave robbery. The beloved disciple sees and believes, though the fullness of resurrection hasn't yet settled in their bones. They return home, but Mary stays. She lingers. She weeps. Her shock and loss are almost too much for her to bear.

It's to her (one dismissed by many, one once broken and restored, one loved and healed by Jesus) that resurrection first speaks. Angels ask her why she weeps. Then a voice behind her: "Why are you weeping? Whom are you looking for?" She thinks it's the gardener, until the person before her calls her by name: "Mary."

That's the first word of resurrection: a name spoken in love. There's something profound in that gesture. Christ rises from the dead, appears to one of the least of his followers (at least in the eyes of the world, but not in the eyes of God), and speaks her name in love. The risen Jesus doesn't begin with proof or power, but with recognition, intimacy, love, and relationship. In that moment, her grief becomes joy, her despair becomes proclamation. She turns from tomb to teacher, from weeping to witness.

"Don't cling to me," he tells her, not because love is withdrawn but because love is expanding. The resurrection means Jesus won't only be with her in flesh but with all who believe, filling the world with presence through the Spirit. This isn't the end of intimacy, but its widening.

Mary runs again, but this time not in grief. She runs with the first gospel sermon: "I've seen the Lord." In her testimony, the church begins. The church is born from the preaching, proclamation, and testimony of a woman. Resurrection proclamation is born not in palaces or courts, but in the tear-streaked face of a woman who loved and lingered.

This passage calls us into that same movement. Resurrection isn't just a past event; it's God's present power breaking into our lives. It meets us in grief and calls us by name. It turns our weeping into witness, our despair into joy. And resurrection reminds us that the kingdom comes not through those the world deems important, but through those who wait, love, and refuse to let go.

When you feel like you are standing before a tomb, remember Mary. Resurrection often begins where tears fall, where hope seems absent, where the gardener whispers your name.

Guiding Truth: Resurrection begins when Jesus calls us by name, turning our weeping into witness and our despair into joy.

Reflection: Where in my life am I standing before a tomb, expecting death rather than life? How is Jesus calling my name, inviting me to turn and see him anew?

Prayer: Risen Lord, speak my name in the places where grief weighs heavily. Please open my eyes to your presence. Turn my mourning into witness. Let me, like Mary, run with joy and declare: "I have seen the Lord." Amen.

Day 47: Peace in the Locked Room

Reading: John 20:19–23

It's evening. Doors are barred. Fear has gathered like a storm inside the disciples' chests. Their Teacher has been crucified, and though whispers of resurrection have reached their ears, terror still outweighs hope. What will the Jewish leaders do to them? What hope and purpose do they have now that their Lord has been crucified? Into this locked room, Jesus comes, not as a ghost, not as a memory, but in risen flesh.

His first word isn't rebuke but blessing: "Peace be with you." This peace isn't the shallow peace of denial, not the brittle quiet of avoidance, but the deep shalom that heals fear, binds wounds, and restores courage. Jesus has always set his eyes on the shalom of God (God's original good intent for all humanity and creation to flourish and know communion with God), and again, Jesus comes with divine peace. Jesus shows them his hands and his side: the marks of crucifixion carried into resurrection. In Christ Jesus, wounds aren't erased; they're glorified. In God made flesh, suffering isn't dismissed; it's transfigured.

Then Jesus says again, "Peace be with you. As the Father has sent me, so I send you." Resurrection isn't only comfort; it's commissioning to be bearers of Jesus's good news of the kingdom of God, and of God's offering of salvation and shalom to all creation and humanity. Jesus doesn't raise them up merely to feel safe but to be sent. The locked room of fear must become the launching ground of mission. As he was sent into the world vulnerable, truthful, and merciful, so now they're sent with the same pattern stamped upon them.

And then comes the gift. Jesus breathes on them: Spirit-breath, creation-breath, shalom-breath, Pentecost before Pentecost. The same Spirit that hovered over the waters at the dawn of creation now hovers over these trembling, fearful disciples. The breath of God fills their lungs, not to inflate egos but to empower forgiveness. "If you forgive the sins of any, they're forgiven." The mission of resurrection is a mission of reconciliation. The Spirit comes not for spectacle but for the slow, daring work of mending a fractured world.

Notice what this means: forgiveness isn't an optional extra. It's the very heart of resurrection life. The disciples aren't authorized to wield swords or build empires; they're entrusted to release captives, heal shame, offer shalom, share divine love, be ambassadors of reconciliation, and announce mercy. Where fear builds walls, forgiveness opens doors. Where shame silences, forgiveness sets free. Where violence reigns, forgiveness declares another kingdom.

This text confronts us still. How many of our rooms are locked by fear? Fear of failure, fear of rejection, fear of uselessness, fear of foolishness, and fear of the world's cruelty. Yet Jesus passes through those walls, not with condemnation but with peace. He breathes on us, too. He sends us, too. And he gives us not the weapons of empire but the power of Spirit-filled forgiveness.

Resurrection isn't only something to celebrate; it's something to embody. To live resurrection life is to live as forgiven and forgiving people and to carry into the world not the stench of fear but the fragrance of peace.

Guiding Truth: The risen Jesus enters our locked rooms with peace, breathes Spirit into us, and sends us into the world as agents of forgiveness.

Reflection: What fears keep me behind locked doors, and how might Jesus be speaking peace into them? How's the Spirit inviting me to embody forgiveness in the places I live and serve?

Prayer: Risen Christ, breathe your Spirit into my fear-filled heart. Please fill me with your peace. Send me where you will. Teach me to forgive as I've been forgiven, and to live as a sign of your resurrection mercy. Amen.

Day 48: The Touch of Faith

Reading: John 20:24–31

Thomas wasn't there when Jesus first appeared. The others told him, breathless, "We have seen the Lord!" But Thomas couldn't anchor his hope in their testimony. He wanted to see, to touch, to place his fingers into the scars of crucifixion. For centuries, we've nicknamed him Doubting Thomas, as if doubt were shameful. But perhaps Thomas gave voice to the honesty many of us suppress. He wanted faith to be tangible. I've often struggled with doubt, only to find that my doubting is a central part of my spirituality and faith, and that this very doubting opens vistas of faith, hope, and love that I never imagined possible.

A week later, Jesus comes again. Same locked doors. Same fearful disciples. But this time, Thomas is present. Jesus turns directly to him, offering the very thing he had asked for: "Put your finger here. See my hands. Reach out your hand and put it in my side. Don't disbelieve but believe."

Notice that Jesus doesn't belittle Thomas, he doesn't scold Thomas for asking, he doesn't recoil from Thomas's humanity. Jesus meets him at the point of his longing. The risen Lord isn't fragile about doubt. He welcomes the questions, the need for proof, the longing for touch. And Thomas, undone by mercy, can only breathe out: "My Lord and my God!" This is the fullest confession of faith in the Gospel of John: born not from abstract argument but from encounter with wounded love.

Jesus then blesses those who won't see in the same way but will still believe. That blessing extends to us. We don't get to touch the scars, but we're invited to trust the testimony, to find Christ in Scripture, in community, in the breaking of bread, in the Spirit's presence. Faith isn't gullibility; it's trust born in relationship, in intimacy with the divine. Jesus blesses those who believe without seeing (a testament to the countless believers across the millennia). Still, he doesn't do this to belittle or dismiss Thomas and his experience of doubt and faith. Jesus meets us and blesses us where we are.

This story rescues us from two errors. On one side, a faith that condemns all doubt, demanding certainty as if questions were betrayal. On the other side, a skepticism that refuses to commit until every answer is airtight. The way of Jesus honors our humanity. He meets our questions with presence, not formulas. He doesn't shame our need but transforms it into confession.

John closes this section by reminding us that these things are written so that we may believe, and in believing, have life in his name. The purpose of the Gospel isn't to satisfy curiosity but to bring us into life. This life isn't one of shallow religion, but a life pulsing with Spirit, grounded in the risen Christ, shaped by wounds turned into glory.

Thomas teaches us that faith isn't the absence of doubt; it's the willingness to bring our doubt to Jesus and let him meet us there. In the end, what matters isn't how strong our faith feels but the One in whom we place it.

Guiding Truth: Jesus meets us in our questions, offering us presence and peace, and calls us into a life-giving faith that confesses him as Lord and God.

Reflection: Where do I need to bring my doubts honestly into the presence of Christ rather than hiding them? How is Jesus inviting me to see and confess him afresh in my daily life?

Prayer: Christ of wounded hands, meet me in my questions. Take my doubt and shape it into trust. Let my confession rise with Thomas: "My Lord and my God." Grant me life in your name, and courage to follow where you lead. Amen.

Day 49: Breakfast at the Shore

Reading: John 21:1–14

The story begins with ordinary failure. The disciples go fishing. All night, nets in the water, sweat on their brows, and nothing to show for it. These are seasoned fishermen, yet they come up empty. It's a haunting image of futility: working with all your strength, casting and recasting, but drawing nothing.

At dawn, a stranger stands on the shore. His voice carries across the water: "Children, have you any fish?" They admit their emptiness. And in that honesty, space is created for grace. Jesus tells them to cast on the right side. The net strains with abundance. The one whom they had failed to recognize is the Lord of their provision.

John says, "It's the Lord." Peter, ever impulsive, throws himself into the water. He can't wait for the boat to reach shore. Love compels him to swim, soaked and shivering, toward the Friend he had once denied.

On the beach, a fire crackles. Fish sizzles. Bread is ready. Jesus doesn't lecture them about their failure or their doubt. He cooks them breakfast. The risen Lord, who conquered death, bends low in hospitality. He feeds hungry bodies before speaking to weary hearts. Here's the gospel in its tenderness: God makes a meal for the empty.

This story reminds us that resurrection isn't abstract. It meets us in fatigue, in failure, in the ordinariness of work that yields nothing. Christ stands at the shoreline of our exhaustion and offers abundance. Not always the abundance of success, but the abundance of presence, nourishment, and grace.

Notice, too, that Jesus invites them to bring some of their own catch. Grace provides, but participation matters. Discipleship is always a joining of divine generosity with human obedience. We bring our small offerings, and Christ transforms them into a shared feast.

This passage also speaks into our culture's obsession with productivity. The disciples worked all night and produced nothing. Jesus, in a single word, fills the net. We're reminded that fruitfulness in the kingdom comes not through endless striving, but through attentive obedience to the voice of Christ. The work is real. The nets must still be thrown. But the abundance comes as gift, not as achievement.

The meal on the shore is Eucharistic in tone. Bread and fish in the hands of the risen Lord become signs of sustenance and communion. This isn't merely breakfast; it's a moment of recognition. They know it's Jesus, though they hardly dare to speak. In the breaking and sharing, presence is revealed.

For us, this story becomes an invitation. To confess our emptiness. To listen for the quiet voice that tells us where to cast again. To swim toward Jesus with reckless longing. To sit at the fire and eat the food he has prepared. And to rise from that meal ready to serve, not in our strength but in his.

Guiding Truth: Christ meets us at the shore of our emptiness, fills us with abundance, and feeds us with grace.

Reflection: Where am I exhausting myself with empty nets instead of listening for Christ's voice? How is Jesus inviting me to receive nourishment before rushing into labor?

Prayer: Risen Lord, meet me at the shoreline of my failure. Call me to cast again at your word. Feed me with your presence. Make me a participant in your abundance and send me out with a heart sustained by your grace. Amen.

Day 50: Restored by Love

Reading: John 21:15–25

I remember reading this passage when I was in my early twenties and thinking, "That's what I want to do. I want to love Jesus and feed his sheep. I want to dedicate my life to feeding and caring for God's people." The story of Jesus's engagement with Peter in this passage gripped my heart and mind and ultimately shaped the rest of my life.

After the fire and the breakfast meal on the shore comes the deeper work. Jesus turns to Peter, the disciple who once swore loyalty but then denied him three times. Now, in the still after breakfast, Jesus asks three times: "Do you love me?" It isn't a coincidence. Each question heals a wound. Each answer stitches back what denial had torn.

The repetition grieves Peter, but this grief is part of the grace. Jesus isn't humiliating him; he's restoring him. The one who faltered is recommissioned: "Feed my lambs. Tend my sheep. Feed my sheep." Love for Jesus must flow outward into care for others. Affection turns into a vocation. Passion becomes pastoral responsibility.

I love the way Jesus meets us in our denial, doubt, brokenness, failings, and sin, and loves us, dignifies us, cleanses us, forgives us, and commissions us.

This moment tells us something vital about discipleship. Failure doesn't disqualify us. Denial isn't the end of the story. Christ restores, recalls, and re-entrusts. The risen Lord doesn't erase Peter's past but redeems it, folding even the failure into the story of grace.

Then Jesus speaks of Peter's future: "When you were young, you dressed yourself and went where you wanted. But when you're old, you'll stretch out your hands, and another will lead you where you don't want to go." John explains this as a reference to Peter's eventual death. The call of discipleship isn't only to feed and serve but also to follow even unto suffering, persecution, and even martyrdom. The one who once denied out of fear will one day give his life in love.

Still, Jesus's words are direct and straightforward: "Follow me." Not "impress me." Not "redeem yourself." Simply humble yourself, follow me, and serve my people. The call is always forward, never chained to the past.

In this final passage of the Gospel, we also see John (the beloved disciple) quietly present. Peter, curious and still comparing, asks about John's fate. Jesus responds: "If I want him to remain until I return, what's that to you? You follow me." Again, the focus is sharpened. Discipleship isn't about rivalry or comparison. Each path is unique, but the command is the same: Follow me.

This is a word we need in our culture of constant measuring, performing, and producing. We compare ministries, lives, successes, and failures. But Jesus cuts through the noise: Don't look sideways. Don't worry about another's journey. Follow me.

The Gospel closes by affirming that Jesus did many other things, too many to record. The story is open-ended, overflowing. It suggests that the presence and work of Christ continue in the lives of those who follow. The book ends, but the story of discipleship continues within us.

Guiding Truth: Jesus restores failures, entrusts them with love's work, and calls each disciple to follow uniquely yet fully.

Reflection: Where do I need to let Christ restore my failures rather than carry them as disqualification? Am I distracted by comparison, or am I listening to the simple call: "Follow me"?

Prayer: Risen Christ, restore the places of my denial with your love. Teach me to tend your sheep with tenderness and courage. Free me from comparison and call me again to follow. Let my whole life be carried in your grace and purpose. Amen.

Appendix 1: Would You Help?

Writing a book takes immense effort. It's a sustained labor of love over months, even years. Every page carries hours of thought, prayer, revision, and hope. And while the writing may be solitary, the life of a book is communal. That's where you come in. If this book has meant something to you, I'd be deeply grateful if you could help it find its way into more hands and hearts.

There are two simple but powerful ways you can do that.

First, consider leaving a short review on Amazon (and Goodreads would be wonderful too). Even just a few sentences can help others discover the book, as reviews significantly influence how books are recommended and shared online. You can do that by visiting Amazon or searching for this book and writing a review. Even a short note helps people find the book.

Second, if the book has stirred something in you, would you share it with others: friends, groups, churches, or anyone who might benefit from its message?

Your support helps keep this work going, and it means more than I can say. Thank you for being part of this journey.

Find this book on these pages:
1. Amazon:
https://www.amazon.com.au/stores/author/B008NI4ORQ
2. Goodreads:
https://www.goodreads.com/author/show/20347171.Graham_Joseph
_Hill
3. Author Website: https://grahamjosephhill.com/books/

Appendix 2: About Me

Graham Joseph Hill (OAM, PhD) is an Adjunct Research Fellow and Associate Professor at Charles Sturt University, and one of Australia's most prolific and awarded Christian authors. He's written more than twenty books, including *Salt, Light, and a City*, which was named Jesus Creed's 2012 Book of the Year (church category); *Healing Our Broken Humanity* (with Grace Ji-Sun Kim), named Outreach Magazine's 2019 Resource of the Year (culture category); and *World Christianity*, shortlisted for the 2025 Australian Christian Book of the Year. In 2024, Graham was awarded the Medal of the Order of Australia (OAM) for his service to theological education. He lives in Sydney with his wife, Shyn.

Author and Ministry Websites

GrahamJosephHill.com

GrahamJosephHill.Substack.com

youtube.com/@GrahamJosephHill_Author

Linktr.ee/dailydevotions

facebook.com/grahamjosephhill/

instagram.com/grahamjosephhill/

amazon.com.au/stores/author/B008NI4ORQ

goodreads.com/author/show/20347171.Graham_Joseph_Hill

Books

See all my books at GrahamJosephHill.com/books

Appendix 3: Connect With Me

I'd love to stay connected with you. You can sign up to my Substack, Spirituality and Society with Hilly, where I share new writing, spiritual reflections, and updates on future books. Please find me on Substack: https://grahamjosephhill.substack.com

You can also find my books on my website: https://grahamjosephhill.com/books

You can also connect with me through my Facebook author page: https://www.facebook.com/GrahamJosephHill/

www.ingramcontent.com/pod-product-compliance
Lightning Source LLC
Chambersburg PA
CBHW031555040426
42452CB00006B/315